VOLNEY P. GAY

READING FREUD
Psychology, Neurosis, and Religion

AAR Studies in Religion 32

READING FREUD

ÆR

American Academy of Religion
Studies in Religion

Charley Hardwick and
James O. Duke, Editors

Number 32

READING FREUD

Psychology, Neurosis, and Religion

by
Volney P. Gay

READING FREUD
Psychology, Neurosis, and Religion

VOLNEY P. GAY

Scholars Press
Chico, California

READING FREUD
Psychology, Neurosis, and Religion

by
Volney P. Gay

© 1983
American Academy of Religion

Library of Congress Cataloging in Publication Data

Gay, Volney Patrick.
  Reading Freud.

  (Studies in religion / American Academy of Religion ;
no. 32)
  1. Psychoanalysis and religion. 2. Freud, Sigmund,
1856–1939. 3. Religion—Controversial literature—History.
I. Title. II. Series: Studies in Religion (American Academy
of Religion) ; no. 32.
BF175.G38 1983   200'.1'9   83–2917
ISBN 0–89130–613–7

Printed in the United States of America

for Barbara

CONTENTS

Acknowledgments

I thank Charley Hardwick and an anonymous reviewer, Peter Homans (University of Chicago), Liston Mills (Vanderbilt), Sarah Gates Campbell (Peabody-Vanderbilt), Norman Rosenblood (McMaster), and Davis Perkins and his colleagues at Scholars Press for their individual efforts on behalf of this book. Every teacher will understand that my greatest debt is to my students. The errors and oversights that remain to be corrected by readers of this book are all my own.

While this book was in final-proof stages I read *A Clinician's Guide to Reading Freud* (New York: Aronson, 1982) by Peter L. Giovacchini. While his title and mine are similar our goals and texts are distinct: he discusses Freud's major treatises on theory. I recommend his book and would place it among the readings listed in the reference section of this book.

INTRODUCTION

Why Study Freud?

Why should students who will live well into the 21st century study the thought of a man who was born just past the midway mark of the 19th? More so, why study the thought of a man whose major doctrines and ideas have been proposed, debated, and judged by numerous authorities and scholars since his first major publications in the 1890s? Finally, have not modern scientists and other authorities refuted those doctrines? The truth of this latter question seems supported by the fact that most professional psychologists and psychiatrists do not consider themselves Freudian in any significant manner.

Yet Freud will not go away. His name and his work still permeate much of the thought of our age, from literary criticism to popular culture. More importantly, there remains a flourishing body of scholars and scientists affiliated with institutes which carry out his basic work.

But the best reason, I believe, for studying Freud is the sheer intellectual joy he affords the serious student. That joy is the pleasure of following a great mind ask and attempt to answer questions of supreme importance to ourselves. Freud's famous essays on childhood sexuality, on dreams, on social relations, and on religion are documents on a heroic scale. They are gripping in their own right. In addition, Freud's intense style and wit give his work a rare literary quality. This fact was recognized when he was awarded the prestigious Goethe Prize for scientific writing.

Finally, people read Freud because they seek to understand themselves. His most famous book, the *Interpretation of Dreams* (1900), is a remarkably open analysis of his own dreams, complete with detailed accounts of the ugly, embarrassing, and petty elements that typify a person's private life. In it Freud aims both to demonstrate the logic of dream interpretation and to show the truths that dreams hide. One cannot read Freud for long without asking oneself the same questions and, under fortunate circumstances, engaging in the same pursuit.

Freud and the Love of Truth

That pursuit is the pursuit of the truth. Ah, but what is truth? When asked this way the question takes on such weight that ordinary mortals cannot hope for much illumination. The truth Freud sought and loved is not the truth of theologians and metaphysicians. Although he too addressed himself to their questions and did not usually denigrate their answers, his route to the problem was radically different. By far the greatest number of questions Freud himself raised appear, when compared to those of religious thinkers, downright trivial. He sought to answer questions that arise from ordinary human complaints: why a young girl falls into sudden and inexplicable faints, or why a young boy wakes up with seemingly endless nightmares about a large animal, or why a graduate student cannot finish her course work.

While these kinds of questions are of vital concern to the individual patients, they do not exercise the minds of great philosophers nor do they pertain to the fate of empires, nor the advance of culture. Yet these questions are the raw material with which Freud worked. Their scientific value lay in their ability to open up an unexplored road to understanding the human mind.

One of Freud's great discoveries was that a person's actions, thoughts, memories, hopes, wishes, fears, and dreams, are of a single piece. Many had said that dreams, for example, were simply the mind working at idle. Freud discovered that dream thoughts were intimately connected to one's deepest feelings and oldest memories. To use one of his favorite metaphors, the psychoanalyst is like an archaeologist who is willing to explore an ancient garbage dump in order to find the pieces that are missing from view. As we will see when we read "Dora," Freud takes this metaphor seriously when he reconstructs, using bits and pieces of material that his patient gives him, not only her history but that of her parents as well. He can do this and hope for success because he believes that every piece will fit together, that every item of behavior is finally the product of forces and motives that one can comprehend.

Discovering the truth about one's "meaningless" actions, therefore, necessarily means that one comes closer to a state of unification, where one understands and can control one's actions. For example, when Dora comes to understand that her coughing is a disguised form of sexual longing, she stops coughing. Does it always work? Does insight into one's actions always bring about this kind of dramatic change? Is psychoanalysis, which is the minute examination of a patient's behavior, always successful? The simplest answer is no. Can insight help promote mental health? Can it provide one with more energy and more strength with which to face ordinary life? Can it serve to free one from terrors and unnameable dread? The simplest answer here is yes.

Freud loved the truth and psychoanalysis is a search for the truth because human beings are, ultimately, unified beings. To put this thought another way, because human beings are unified, because every action is finally meaningful, falsehood in one area of one's life, like sexuality, distorts necessarily the whole of one's life. In Freud's language, when we distort the truth about ourselves we sabotage our most vital ability, the ability to distinguish true and false. Even petty lies, boasts, small deviousnesses, are costly because we distort both our memory and our natural capacity to distinguish the truth. Because a person is a whole, unified being, even if he or she feels otherwise, lying is a self-inflicted wound. One may easily verify this claim by recalling, in strictest privacy, some past event in which one was a little humiliated or defeated in some measure, and then trying to reconstruct the exact sequence of events: who said what, how one stumbled, etc. It is much easier to recall one's victories than to recall one's defeats, unless those defeats were so great that one can now think of nothing else!

This leads us to a final question. If lying to oneself is so costly, if it impairs the ego, why do it? The obvious answer is because it helps reduce the amount of psychical pain outright. Lying is effective, especially in the short run when an angry parent, for example, is searching for the child who ruined his book. As one matures one lies less often. Rather one learns to prevaricate, distort, fib, equivocate, and also to pervert, misrepresent, slant, twist, whitewash and otherwise stretch the truth in order to protect oneself.

The Goals of This Book

The primary goal of this short book is to interrogate systematically Freud's major essays on religion. To do that well requires us to know what he is talking about when he compares religious rituals, for example, to obsessional actions. And to understand those kinds of comparisons we must understand his general theory of personality and character. There are many excellent texts that summarize, criticize, and develop Freud's general theory. In the course of this handbook I will refer to them as well as to other relevant studies. However, none of them is quite like this handbook because none of them is written in the interrogative mode.

I have chosen to structure this handbook around a series of question sheets because they permit me to reach my second, pedagogical goal: to illuminate how Freud thinks, not simply document what he thinks. The chapters that follow might be seen as scaffolds erected alongside Freud's texts. I have tried to plant them square and near enough the edifice so that we can study it with care. But just as a good mason does not confuse the scaffolding with the original building, so too we will not confuse these chapters on Freud's thought with Freud or psychoanalysis itself.

My third goal is to elucidate the way Freud understood religion: it is an almost-good-enough attempt to promote human happiness. Freud's understanding of religion is essentially tragic. Like the hero of classic tragedy, religion is an entity that is noble but inherently flawed, tainted by birth, and incapable of adjusting to the real world of ordinary mortals.

A final introductory question: Why not just read Freud's own book, *The Future of an Illusion*, and forego these other texts? It would seem to contain his clearest opinions about religion. This is so. It is a clear, well-written summary of his major opinions about the nature of religion and about its faults and its virtues. *The Future of an Illusion* contains Freud's opinions about religion, but it does not permit us to see how he arrived at those opinions.

Freud claims consistently that psychoanalysis is a science of the mind. If so, it is more than a philosophical system, or a set of religious insights, or a moral code that one can comprehend only aesthetically. A science is a method of inquiry into the truth of things. It can be transmitted from teacher to student. It can be criticized and developed by subsequent thinkers.

If Freud is correct in claiming that psychoanalysis is a science, then we should be able to reconstruct the reasoning that produced his particular judgments, whether those judgments are about neuroses or about religion itself. More so, a science should allow one to advance beyond the discoveries of its originater. Its future must be more than the future of an illusion. The debate about the scientific nature of psychoanalysis is still raging. For our purposes I will assume that that question remains open and that we can therefore set out on the seas of Freud's thought.

What This Book Will Not Do

First, and most obvious, it will not serve as an introduction to all of Freud's thought. I have not focused any questions on two immense areas in his writings: the theory of technique, which includes questions of therapy and cure, and the theory of mind, which includes questions of metapsychological explanations.

The theory of psychoanalytic technique, how one engages the patient, overcomes resistances, and initiates the curative process, is indirectly related to Freud's critique of religion. There are fascinating connections between psychoanalytic cure, for example, and ritual confession. But I see no way to make those connections clear without a lengthy excursion into Freud's general theory of therapy.

Freud's metapsychology is another kettle of fish. Where the essays on therapy require one to examine one's actual behavior, and ideally one's behavior under analysis, the essays on metapsychology are purely theoretical treatises that attempt to account for psychoanalytic observations. In a somewhat oversimplified sense, the metapsychology is to the clinical theory as linguistics is to learning how to read. One may take part in the analytic process, as patient or therapist, just as one may read easily without recourse to theory of how those processes occur.

How to Use This Book

The Standard Edition of the Complete Psychological Works of Sigmund Freud (hereafter referred to as the Standard Edition or SE) has 23 volumes of text and a single volume of indexes. These contain more than 7,000 pages or roughly about four and a half million words. No one is going to read or comprehend them in a single term of college level work.

This book should be used as one might employ a local guide to a foreign country about which one knows little. Just as there are many ways to explore England, so too there are many ways to explore the Standard Edition. My route has three major links: (1) an overview, (2) Freud on psychic pain, and (3) the analysis of religion. I have tried to make each of these links both independent of every other, and yet reasonably tied together so that one might read the sections in order. If you are by yourself on this trip you may well choose to linger where a group of classmates or teacher might not.

If this book is used in a class I believe it might serve to supplement a teacher's lectures and perhaps serve as a guide to independent study. Of course it might also serve as an opponent against which one may contend and triumph. I have used these kinds of question sheets myself for seven years or so and I am now addicted to them. My hope is that they will serve both teachers and students and help them take up one of the greatest challenges afforded us, a conversation with Freud.

References and Texts

All my Freud references are to the Standard Edition. Some teachers and many students will not have immediate access to these 24 volumes (though any university library should have them). However, I work through each text systematically, using Freud's chapter headings as my major subheadings. Hence one can follow my questions even if one has a text the page numbers of which do not correspond to those of the SE. Each of the texts I discuss is available in good paperback editions.

The core psychoanalytic literature, including major books and psychoanalytic journals, is much larger than 100,000 items. An ideal handbook would cross-reference those items to these questions and so give the reader a truly useful map to this immense literature. But this is not an ideal text. Given the confines of severe page limitations I can only list a minimal research literature in the appendix. The reference section has four parts: Freud's work; texts on Freud the man; texts on the history and theory of psychoanalysis; and a list of prominent psychoanalytic journals.

I

FREUD'S LECTURES ON PSYCHOANALYSIS
Five Lectures on Psycho-Analysis (SE 11) 1909
Introductory Lectures on Psycho-Analysis
(SE 15 & 16) 1915–1917

Freud was one of the very best expositors of psychoanalysis (spelled "psycho-analysis" only in the SE). He was keenly aware of the public's fascination with his science and he recognized the value of keeping them informed about it. Hence he took great care in composing popular lectures. (For additional information on introductions to psychoanalytic thought and therapy see the texts listed in the appendixes.)

Five Lectures on Psycho-Analysis
(SE 11) 1909

Though very brief and when compared to the *Introductory Lectures* of 1916–1917, of less stature, these five short lectures are an excellent overview of the major points Freud will pursue in the longer, and more technical series. One can read them at one sitting and so gain a beginning orientation to the subject matter at hand.

First Lecture

Technical Terms

Trauma; absence; hysterical paralysis; conscious and unconscious; "talking cure"; affect; suppression; displacement

1   Every reasonable reader will wonder how the physician or therapist is able to tell whether or not a patient's symptoms are caused by physical factors, emotional ones, or a combination of the two types. Does Freud help us with this question? One clue is that symptoms produced by emotional shock would seem to be primarily psychological and hence treatable by psychological means (p. 10). Is this sufficient in every case?

2   What was it about Anna O.'s states of "absence" that demonstrated they were produced by psychological causes? Were her

actions during the states of "absence" causally related to previous experiences? When Breuer began to treat her symptoms he used hypnosis to induce a synthetic state of "absence." Why would this seem a reasonable method to follow?

3   ". . . Our hysterical patients suffer from reminiscences" (p. 16) is a famous statement taken from Freud's and Breuer's joint book, *Studies on Hysteria* (SE 2). Strictly speaking, is it true? That is, is it merely the accurate memory of a painful event in their past which haunts them or something additional? Note that Freud adds the phrase "mnemic symbols" to his fuller explication of this dictum. Why is that a more adequate summary of his claim?

4   How does he argue from the clinical observations of Anna's "double conscience" to a theorem about conscious and unconscious mental states? What evidence can he offer to suggest that an "unconscious" mental state can influence a conscious mental state in a normal person? Is Freud's goal to erect a theory of pathology only?

5   The last paragraph in this lecture ought to be read very slowly and with great care. If we are fortunate we will understand it now, at the beginning, and recall it when Freud's exposition becomes complex and, sometimes, contradictory.

     This is another way of saying that Freud feels it is a mark of his scientific goals and scientific honesty that his accounts are often incomplete and his theories subject to change without notice. This makes the task of his readers (and expositors) especially difficult. Why should we, therefore, learn to suspect a theoretician whose account is full, complete, and rigorously deductive?

Second Lecture

Technical Terms

Dissociation; resistance repression; pressure technique; dynamic; substitute symptoms; sublimation

6   Freud studied with some of the most famous psychiatrists in Europe. For the most part, he says, they searched for physiological explanations of mental disorders like hysteria. So did Freud. Yet he gave up that particular hope. What observations were crucial to that decision? How did the success of the "pressure technique" demonstrate that he could forego the concept of "absence" and no longer had to hypnotize his patients?

7   What is the sequence of clinical trials that gave rise to the concept of "resistance" (p. 24)? Is this concept a clinical observation or clinical generalization? That is, would any neutral observer of such patients come to agree with Freud's use of this term?

8   To illustrate this central concept and its relationship to the equally important one of repression, Freud uses an analogy drawn from a public event, namely, his lecture. Why is this an especially apt choice, given what we know of the doctor–patient relationship Freud experienced during the period he employed the pressure technique? Compare the metaphors Freud used to describe intrapsychic conflict with the metaphors and models Breuer, Charcot, and Bernheim and even Anna O. herself used to describe hysteria.

9   Why does he say that the concept of "repression" is only the beginning of a psychological theory (p. 26) and not the conclusion? How is repression an essentially "dynamic" concept? What underlying implications does this term have, especially given its etymology, for Freud's general orientation to psychological theory?

10   A "symptom" is a substitute for the repressed idea (p. 27). What is the implied analogy here? Can physical symptoms of organic diseases be said to have representatives or to act as substitutes? If neurotic symptoms are, as Freud says, capable of forming substitutes can one predict which behaviors or thoughts or dream images a particular kind of patient will manifest in his or her treatment? Is psychoanalysis a kind of history or a kind of empirical investigation of unchanging patterns of psychological function?

Third Lecture

Technical Terms

Word Association Test; complex; free associations; psychological determinism; dream work; manifest dream and latent dream thoughts; condensation and displacement

11   Freud's gentle irony about his prejudice (p. 29) deserves careful consideration. On what grounds did he proceed to tell his patients that even while awake, that is, not under hypnosis, every one of their thoughts (their associations) would prove of value to the analysis. At first, he says, this was confirmed by the obvious paths their thoughts took. But eventually their associations became more and more tenuous. Why was it a mistake for him to agree with these (initial) patients and reject these latter kind of associations?

12   His adherence to the principle of psychological determinism permits him to explain why some associations are only apparently irrelevant to the precipitating trauma. How? How does his explanation of severely distorted associations fit into a comprehensive dynamic psychology?

13   Once again, to illustrate an especially important—and original— part of his theory he uses an analogy, a joke, drawn not from

science, but from a rather complex social interaction (pp. 30–31). In the joke it was the wit and skill of the connoisseur that permitted him to make the allusion to the Savior on which the entire story turns. Given Freud's analogy, to which aspect of the mind (sometimes termed the "mental apparatus") must we then assign skills of a similar nature?

14   The analysis of associations, of dreams, and of parapraxes serves the psychoanalyst in his or her attempt to discover the unconscious (pp. 32–33). What are the patient's responsibilities in the enterprise (according to Freud in this text at this time)?

15   Are most people skeptical of the claims psychoanalysts make about the unconscious motives that animate us all? Psychoanalysis is a science that emerged through the treatment of "nervous" patients by medical doctors. What has it got to do with people like ourselves? Why are dreams so important to Freud's presentation and to his general theory?

16   How are we, his listeners and readers, akin to neurotics, and even perverts and profoundly disturbed psychiatric patients? What fact of our daily life, one to which most of us have immediate access, is a replica of all these mental disturbances? What is "sufficiently wonderful" (p. 34) about dreams themselves?

17   To how many things may the term "dream" refer as it is used in ordinary conversation? And to how many distinct mental contents does Freud's use of the term refer? Which of the terms, manifest dream or latent dream thoughts, refers to the "dream-like" product with which we are most familiar?

18   Freud says the analysis of dreams is the royal road to understanding the unconscious functioning of the mind. Why is it also the road that permits him, a dream interpreter, to understand neurotic symptoms? How does the technical term "repression" help him explain both irrational dream imagery and irrational neurotic symptoms? How is the "dream-work" (an odd enough term) related to repression?

19   On p. 36 Freud uses technical terms (condensation, displacement, sublimations, reaction formation) without defining them or giving examples. He will do both later on in the *Introductory Lectures*, to which we turn after this section. Yet one can make a rough approximation of their meaning by comparing them to those terms which have opposite meanings. (And what are those?)

20   Freud then turns to discuss "faulty actions" or as his English translators call them, "parapraxes." Most people, he says, are perfectly aware of such events or actions and yet almost always consider them to be meaningless, as if they were accidents. Which great principle of psychoanalytic theory does this opinion violate?

21 If Freud is correct in his assessment of one's usual response to parapraxes—that is, that one brands them as pointless accidents—why must one analyze one's own examples? This call to examine one's own life in light of psychoanalytic claims is unavoidable. It enrages and even disgusts many people who feel Freud is not playing fair, as it were, philosophically, to force them to assume the validity of his most contentious claims. Yet which element of his general theory requires us to engage in a minimum of self-analysis?

22 What does the "arrogance of consciousness" (p. 39) mean? If Freud is correct, it means that we too, as students of his thought, cannot understand him fully without analyzing our own parapraxes, and, eventually, our dreams. In attempting this kind of analysis it may help if you keep notes on a day-to-day basis (though once the topic of parapraxes is introduced and explained in a public forum there emerge suddenly numerous "Freudian slips," often committed by the lecturer).

Fourth Lecture

Technical Terms

Libido; instincts (drives); fixation; regression; nuclear complex; perversions; pregenital sexuality; object choice; erotogenic zones

23 Freud is famous for his theories of childhood sexuality, most of which are misrepresented when they appear in short chapters in psychology textbooks. How did he come to place so much emphasis on sexual (or erotic) factors in the development of children, and, later, in the development of neurotic conditions in adults? Why does he say he was "converted" to the libido theory only later (p. 40)?

24 What can he mean by the phrase "under the spell of the combination of prudery and prurience" which he says typifies the attitude most adults have toward sexuality? Is this true in our "modern" age too? Give an example of this combination in a contemporary setting. If one can find no such illustrations how do you account for the discrepancy between Freud's judgment of his time and your findings?

25 When he raises the issue of childhood sexuality (p. 41) he is ready for a stream of abuse and condemnation. Would his findings arouse the same sentiments in our times? What is the standard "modern" opinion about childhood sexuality now? Can we distinguish between that "manifest" opinion, as it is expressed in newspapers and baby-books, like that of Dr. Spock, and "latent" opinions on the

same subject? What kinds of observations would be required to make such a comparison a valid and convincing one?

26 If people bother to think of childhood sexuality at all, they usually conceive it as a single kind of behavior, involving the genitals, modeled on adult (heterosexual) intercourse. Why is this "adultomorphic" opinion wrong, according to Freud's research? How many sexual instincts (or "drives") are there operating in the child?

27 Why does he say that children have a "dissociated" sexual life that is brought to order only after puberty—and sometimes not ever? And why, according to his summary on p. 44, must we conclude that whatever the number of component instincts or pregenital instincts the total will always be an even number?

28 This entire discussion of childhood sexuality is schematic and therefore not fully persuasive. Among its least clear statements is the assertion about "coprophilia" (p. 45). (Although he does not say it here or on the preceding page, this kind of interest or compulsion ought to be subsumed under anal, pregenital trends.) Surely this is a disgusting topic, one pertinent only to the most esoteric of psychiatric specialities—hardly worth mentioning in a distinguished setting like that of Clark University or to a group of refined readers.

It is true that most (adult) people do not manifest warm and accepting feelings toward their feces, nor toward other bodily products, like sputum, nor toward that of others. But is anality a rare event exhibited only in the actions of the very ill? Consider the range of obscene terms which employ anal allusions—why are they so popular and so powerful?

29 Since all adults have been children, and all children manifest infantile sexuality, it follows that all adults will have had to surmount those earlier, pregenital trends (usually by repression) in order to achieve adult, genital sexuality. If trouble then occurs in their sexual life, "the repression that took place during the course of development will be broken through at the precise points at which infantile fixations occurred" (p. 46). Why? What metaphor or model underlies this image of infantile sexuality "breaking through" the repression barrier? (Note the entire set of metaphors which Freud employs to describe the intermingling of pregenital trends.)

30 You may be struck by Freud's use of the term "object," as on p. 47 where he speaks of the child's first choice of an object to love. It would appear that this technical term means merely "person"—so why does he persist in using "object"? Either he is trying for and achieving a measure of obscurity or he uses the term for a particular reason. And what might that be? (Note that pregenital sexual

trends, the original collection of diverse "instincts," also have objects, or, better, "objectives.")

31 To which set of mental factors—intellectual capacities or sexual interests—does Freud ascribe dominance? In his discussion of the nuclear complex, which he was to rename shortly the Oedipus complex, he says that even after it is repressed it continues to exert influence upon the child's life. How does he explain the persistence of most implausible theories of birth in children who are otherwise observant, intelligent, and well educated?

32 Finally, he says children must struggle to free themselves from their nuclear complex (p. 48). Is this merely a manner of speaking, to give added clarity to his contention about the Oedipus complex? What aspects of the theory of repression, including our own knowledge of the feelings with which it is usually associated, support Freud's choice of words? Is the task of separating a child from its original erotic ties to its parents a matter for moral exhortation or something else?

Fifth Lecture

Technical Terms

Regression; sublimation; transference; "flight into illness"; condemnation

This is an extremely condensed lecture, summarizing as it does not just the previous four, but nearly twenty years of work. It contains a number of precise formulations. It will be worth our time to ponder them slowly.

33 In the first paragraph Freud gives a causal explanation of neurosis: because people are frustrated in one realm they retreat to another where they find "satisfaction" (p. 49). What does he mean by satisfaction? Are not neurotics miserable, anxious, sometimes depressed, and sometimes impossibly happy, that is, manic? Are neurotics aware of any distinct form of satisfaction brought about by their symptoms? (Are not symptoms defined as conscious complaints?)

34 The "flight into illness" follows along what two paths? He says that this flight back to earlier, erotic modes of satisfaction *is* the illness and responsible for the "main damage caused by it." In what does this kind of damage consist? That is, what parts of the person are harmed necessarily by these regressions that give rise to neurotic suffering (and to neurotic pleasures)?

35 How is modern neurosis like an ancient monastery (this is Freud's wonderful analogy that reads almost like a joke)? Are we all liable to the onset of a neurotic condition? Broadly speaking, what two

factors must operate together in a person's circumstances such that neurosis is the outcome? Given Freud's comments about fixation and regression, above, to what kinds of facts would one require access in order to predict both the type of neurosis that would follow and the unconscious fantasies that would accompany it?

36 Why is transference (p. 51) a "strange phenomenon"? Note that when we read and discuss his actual case histories, below, Freud will confess that he failed many times in his early career because he had no understanding of transference. He gives us only a brief definition in this lecture. Transference occurs when a patient exhibits strong feelings, both positive and negative, toward the therapist. These are repetitions of earlier (now unconscious) feelings and fantasies about former love objects. But why did he not predict the existence of such feelings, say, at least by the late 1890s when he was composing *The Interpretation of Dreams* (1900a)? In other words, why is psychoanalysis not a predictive science?

37 Freud seems especially concerned to explain not just what his theories are but to explain why they are so often despised. He offers two distinct reasons for their unpopularity (at least in 1909). One is that people fear it may harm them since it obviously deals with intimate and often painful topics. Second, most people do not accept the principle of determinism (p. 52). Are these two fears connected by a more profound anxiety? (Consider the common understanding of the power that unconscious wishes hold—can one link these anxieties about unconscious processes to aspects of religious life?)

38 On the same page he gives one of his early formulas as to the aim of psychoanalytic treatment. According to this formula what is the therapist's role once the unconscious wishes have emerged, through symptoms, or parapraxes, or dreams? What would a condemning judgment look like? (Would religion be of help at any stage in the treatment process?)

39 In addition to condemnation, there are two other outcomes possible: sublimation and active satisfaction of the infantile wish. We will see him return to the first concept again and again in his essay on religion (and in the case histories, too) where he gives his readers a much more useful description of this process. Must all infantile sexual wishes, about which we his readers still know very little, come under the dominance of the genital organization in mature, heterosexual life? Can they? How does sublimation operate such that repression does not take place? (If we cannot answer this kind of question at this point, what kind of information would we need, and what concepts would require clarification, before we could?)

40 Freud leaves his audience with a humorous story about clever folk who demand more and more sacrifices from a once mighty animal. He says some may consider it an exaggerated, even if clever, warning. Is it? The horse died, an event that would put an end to its usefulness and cause the townsfolk some consternation since they had lost a very valuable property. Is there a corresponding clarity in the case of children and the demands made upon them to conform to idealized social norms? How could one measure these kinds of costs? And who would feel them most? Who would feel them least?

Introductory Lectures on Psycho-Analysis
(SE 15 & 16) 1915–1917

As the editor of this volume tells us, Freud prepared these lectures for delivery to an educated audience beginning in October of 1915. Since that audience is very similar to that for which this book is intended, it will pay us to read them slowly and with care. Where Freud had used the *Five Lectures* to describe his science to an elite group of scholars, he uses these longer lectures to persuade a more general audience whose skepticism he anticipates with neither apology nor rancor.

I have divided these 28 lectures into three parts: (1) Introduction and Parapraxes, (2) Dreams and Dream Interpretation, and (3) Human Development and Therapy. Questions in each section are numbered independently.

PART ONE

Lecture I: Introduction

1 Why does Freud "seriously advise" his readers that they may not appreciate the way he intends to treat them (p. 15)? No doubt you have read or heard about psychoanalysis already. Does annoyance appear to be a typical response people have to psychoanalysis itself?

2 "One learns psycho-analysis on oneself, by studying one's own personality" (p. 19). Is this typical of scientific disciplines? He says one advances even further by becoming a patient of a trained analyst. Why might this be so? If Freud is correct does that mean that critics of psychoanalysis must themselves also undergo an analysis?

3 On pp. 21–24 he lists the two great "insults" his science perpetrates: one about the unconscious, the other about sexuality. Why are these insulting? What kinds of things do most people find insulting? An insult is an affront to one's positive understandings

of oneself or one's group. Given this, what kinds of feelings must psychoanalytic patients experience as they undergo treatment?

4 He then offers a condensed explanation of why his science arouses such intense feelings (an explanation that prefigures his essays on religion). Why must society condemn his labors? Must this be true of all societies or just "Victorian" epochs like that of the late 19th century?

Lecture II: Parapraxes

5 Freud himself did not use the word "parapraxes," a term which his English translators concocted out of two Greek words: "para" (along or beside) and "praxis" (action or behavior). Why would they make up pseudo-Greek terms like this? Why not use English words like "faulty action"?

6 Whatever the reason, note that Freud calmly assures his audience that everyone, not just his patients, experiences parapraxes. Why does he choose to begin with this kind of fact? Why not begin with a description of one of the more outlandish case histories available to him? He had no lack of sensational anecdotes, full of sexual actions, the descriptions of which could not fail to interest an audience. Yet he begins his exposition with an account of "mis-hearing," "missaying," and other parapraxes. Why this subdued subject at this point? (Can you predict with what tone he might begin a private analysis?)

7 Is it true we instinctively trust "small pointers" (pp. 26–28), especially nonverbal messages, when assessing a person's true feelings toward us? Can one lie as easily in either mode: verbally as well as nonverbally? Note that he uses a curious analogy: that of the detective and the murderer. Why that analogy at this juncture? Who, in the analytic situation, is the detective, who the murderer?

8 ". . . Everything is related to everything, including small things to great" (p. 27). What does this mean for the psychological investigator? If true, would it be a source of comfort and solace for the therapist presented with a puzzling case?

9 Freud then argues against purely physiological explanations for parapraxes, especially slips of the tongue. Why must he do so? Note that he invokes the authority of two great dramatists (pp. 36–39). Why would he turn to artists as sources of confirmation of his theory rather than to the scientists of his day?

Lecture III: Parapraxes

10 Freud's central claim is that "slips" are not accidents or happenstance occurrences made in a random way. Rather he says they

can be interpreted as meaningful utterances in their own right. How? That is, on what grounds can we "guess the second intention" (p. 43)? Can intentions of this second kind—the unconscious kind—be as diverse and complex as conscious ones? If so, Freud says psycho-physiological explanations are empty phrases (p. 46). Why? (Note that the criminal elements return in his example.)

11 Freud's examples of linguistic slips are mainly German. To assess his general theory and his general claims—claims that are typical of "every psycho-analytic investigation" (p. 48)—one must use real examples taken from real life. Describe two or three examples. Do they show the dual structure that Freud says all parapraxes must have?

12 "You will break off at that point, but only to take up your resistance again at another point" (p. 49). What does resistance mean here? The interchange becomes heated—are the judicial metaphors essential parts of the argument now?

Lecture IV: Parapraxes

13 This last chapter on parapraxes summarizes the others. In it Freud expands the notion of two trains of thought to cover instances of forgetting, losing articles, etc. His method is to "interpret" the faulty action or the failure to carry out the intended one. Is the correct interpretation always obvious? Are there constraints upon interpretations like this? What might "wild psychoanalysis" be?

14 Freud has led us to one of his basic principles: ". . . mental life is the arena and battle-ground for mutually opposing purposes . . ." (p. 76). How do the adjectives "conscious" and "unconscious" pertain to this claim? Is the "battle" pleasant or unpleasant? If the latter, what must characterize the patient's experience within psychoanalysis?

PART TWO

Lecture V: Dreams— Difficulties and First Approaches

1 Is Freud comparing apples and oranges when he starts, right off the bat, with equating dreams and neurotic symptoms? Note that he puts the usual objections smack into the open (pp. 83–84). Why be so blatant? Why does "an excess of criticism" (p. 84) make him suspicious?

2 Why is he not keen on the "exact sciences" (p. 87) and their investigations of dreams? He then addresses dreams and sleep. Why does the world "not possess even those of us who are adults completely"

(p. 88)? Is a dreamless sleep the best kind of sleep? (Why did Hamlet fear that sleep that may come after death?)

3 He says there are at least two features common to all dreams: they are produced by the mind while asleep, and they differ qualitatively from ordinary thinking (p. 90). Is a third feature their "meaningfulness"? Freud's initial answer is no. But is this his opinion at the end of the chapter?

4 As usual, he considers reasonable objections to his line of inquiry: for example, some dreams are quite ordinary and even "undreamlike." Yet will they yield to interpretation as well? He rejects the academic psychologists and sides with the common wisdom, especially that embedded in ordinary language. Why is the term "daydream" a "hint"? Is this a fourth common feature?

Lecture VI: The Premises
and Technique of Interpretation

5 This is the bridge chapter between the analysis of parapraxes and the interpretation of dreams. Page 101 is the keystone of that bridge. If dreams mean something, why can we not simply ask the dreamer what that meaning is? Freud sees fit to use a rare exclamation point. Why?

6 Again, he summarizes the obvious criticisms against his position. What are those and how does he handle them? Why does he emphasize the importance of not concealing these difficulties, especially to a naive audience?

7 But he does offer some corroboration in the form of a report on hypnotic treatment. Given that analogy, who is the hypnotist, who the subject, and what provides the content in the interpretation of a patient's dreams?

8 The exclamation points multiply rapidly on p. 105 where he describes the "lively opposition" to his technique: what is the major complaint raised against his method? And why is Freud so sure that his simple method—asking the dreamer to report the first thoughts that occur—must work?

9 Is "free association" really free (p. 106)? If it were perfectly free, that is, uncaused and unpredictable by any means, could Freud's method work? He mentions some experiments—some that you can carry out, like his young patient described on p. 107.

10 He says his method assumes that a person's thoughts will eventually lead to the "complex" which he or she has. What is a "complex," according to this text? Is it distinct from what we ordinarily call "character"?

11 The experience of forgetting a name and struggling to recall it is

an especially good illustration of the work of dream analysis (pp. 110–111). Why is he so fond of the term "work"? Is the example on these pages simple?

Lecture VII: The Manifest Content of Dreams and the Latent Dream-Thoughts

12 Freud summarizes his argument on p. 113 and introduces the term "substitutive structures." (We shall see this term reappear in the essays on culture.) He then lists three rules (pp. 114–115) and, on p. 117, adds a fourth principle about the level of resistance. There is an immense literature on psychoanalytic interpretations (see the appendixes below). What is the most likely objection to them? He says, "We must wait till the concealed unconscious material we are in search of emerges of its own accord" (p. 114), exactly as did the word "Monaco." Is this analogy between dream interpretation and recalling a word "on the tip of one's tongue" perfectly consistent?

13 What prevents any crazy "interpretation" from becoming as defensible as any other? Note that if Freud cannot answer this question the remainder of his claims are simply so much smoke. As usual he is ahead of us, for in the next paragraph he mentions the importance of self-analysis. Why is that so important? To hone our skills? Or to realize—and so gain conviction—that we too have an inner, unconscious resistance?

14 Freud's tone changes in the next page when he lists the "rules" and "promises" he extracts from his dreamer (and his patients). Why this change? How does the existence of so many examples of "disobedience" validate his technique of interpretation and his claims about the unconscious?

15 Freud's examples and metaphors are always important aspects of his argument, e.g., that on p. 116. If a patient's associations lead to an image of himself as an especially fine person, or another patient's associations lead to an image of herself as a loving daughter, are these the core "latent dream thoughts"? How do we know they cannot be the deepest layer of the dream?

16 By now you will have found that Freud pretty much inverts the usual understanding of dreams and dream meanings. Why, given his method and his theory, must it follow that perfectly normal dreams are necessarily products of the most intense distortion?

17 In this chapter Freud has revealed his full hand, demonstrated his argument, and fulfilled the expectations of his enemies: he dismisses their criticisms of psychoanalytic theory unless they too have undergone an analysis. Why would Freud demand this even

of the most educated and expert scientists of his day? What other disciplines demand a similar initiation?

Lecture VIII: Children's Dreams

18   Here Freud begins to gather in his generalizations about dreams, using those of children as examples. The most important conclusion, and one only hinted at earlier, is number 6: a wish is the motive force behind the dream (p. 129). How does this momentous claim allow him to link the interpretation of dreams with the interpretation of parapraxes?

19   He then asks a profound question: Why have other authorites not recognized that all dreams are, at some level, the expression of a wish? The answer is suggested by his remark, "We can well imagine what it is that has held them back . . ." (p. 131). And what is that thing?

Lecture IX: The Censorship of Dreams

20   Like the brilliant novelist who only alludes to the unhappy fate a character will suffer, Freud has led us up to this central chapter. Like the herald in a Greek play, he announces his theme again in the first paragraph: only those dreams that are the hallucinated fulfillment of a wish are completely intelligible. What is the corollary principle, therefore, regarding interpretation?

21   He uses another new term, "the dream work" (p. 136). What is this? And why, again, does he use the term work? Why does he say that the old lady condemned the dream and that this is a sign she understood how to interpret it?

22   From where does he draw the term "dream censor"? Does this entity or agency operate in one mode only? Or many? Can one predict the number of ways it might reach its goals?

23   Is the censorship fixed or does it change? What kinds of events in one's life will alter the amount of sexual and aggressive themes that emerge in one's dreams? If Freud is correct about the censorship, what kinds of feelings will one experience upon hearing the correct interpretation of a heavily censored dream?

24   Whose wishes are those that analysis uncovers? An inner being? A hidden, interior personality? Why does he refer to the Great War (World War I) at this juncture in the debate? How does the existence of evil figure into his last enigmatic remarks on a part of the mind that is "permanently unconscious " (p. 148)?

Lecture X: Symbolism in Dreams

Since his publication of *The Interpretation of Dreams* in 1899, Freud's name has been linked to a set of symbols of sexual matters to such a degree that the odd knife, cigar, and water-tower, like the odd cave, trap-door, and valley, are termed "Freudian symbols." This chapter is a condensed discussion of chapter VI of *The Interpretation of Dreams*.

25   Note that the nature of dream symbols is described by way of the failure of free-association (p. 149). Why is this a necessary element in Freud's presentation? Is his a "timid" experiment (p. 150)? How is free-association the inverse method of interpretation to those of "dream books"? Which method is central to the psychoanalytic enterprise?

26   He then lists a set of typical symbols: objects which invariably represent something else. Why are they so monotonous? He also refers to old jokes, folklore, and "buffoonery," as other areas in which one can see sexual symbols operating in the open. If these symbols are of so obvious and banal a nature, why does Freud claim to be saying something new about dream life when he mentions them in this context?

27   He hurries through the listing of the symbols in order to speak about an "ancient" language (pp. 166–167). Are these speculations essential to his argument?

28   The central question for Freud was why are dreams, sometimes, so obscure. Symbols may be partly to blame. Are they the most important source of obscurity and craziness in dreams?

Lecture XI: The Dream-Work

The most important sentence of this chapter is the first line of the second paragraph: ". . . We were studying the relations between the elements of dreams and the genuine things they stood for." As Freud notes it is easy to misunderstand him. The concept of dream-work is one of his most original notions: from it or upon it he erected much of his theory of neurosis, and, in turn, upon that theory he erected his theory of culture.

29   How many dreams are there to be considered whenever a manifest dream is reported? What is the actual work that the dream-work accomplishes? (Again, note Freud's penchant for the notion of work as applied to psychological processes.)

30   He says there is a strict relationship between the way the dream-work constructs the manifest dream and the way in which the interpreter must reconstruct the latent dream-thoughts. What is this relationship? If this claim is valid, why would it therefore

make sense to say that the art of interpretation is a kind of anti-censorship (p. 70)?

31   Freud then lists three "achievements" that the dream-work accomplishes in the course of creating the manifest dream. Why are these three—condensation, displacement, visualization—called "achievements"? As usual he asks his readers to recall their own dream examples in order to verify the presence of each of these achievements.

32   He says condensation may serve the goals of distorting the latent dream thoughts—since it may make the dream more obscure—but it is not an "effect of the dream-censorship" (p. 173). Is it exactly like translation from one language to another? If not, then to what shall we liken it? (Note that if the translation/transcription metaphors fail to impress us, Freud's request to examine actual cases of condensation takes on more urgency.)

33   Displacement, the second achievement, is "entirely the work of the dream-censorship" (p. 174). How do we know this? That is, what characteristics of displacement make it purely a function of the censorship? (Note his allusion to the mechanisms of jokes vs. that of displacement in dreams.)

34   The third achievement he calls "transforming thoughts into their visual images"—a long-winded term. In other texts he calls this symbolization. But is this third mode akin to the symbolic substitutions he described in chapter 10? Which parts of speech are easiest to visualize? And which are the most difficult to visualize? Is this third mode like displacement—that is controlled by the censorship? Or is it like condensation—a product of thought processes that cannot represent logical relations like "because"?

35   He then makes one of his most famous and provocative claims: ". . . A representation of 'no'—or at any rate an unambiguous one—is not to be found in dreams" (p. 178). What kind of logical relation is entailed by the concept of "no"? That is, what minimal rules of either language or logic must one employ in order to use correctly a sign meaning "no"?

36   How is the inability to represent "no" related to the fact that contraries may signify their opposites in dreams? If the latent dream-thoughts exemplify myriad contradictions, and cannot express negation, are they capable of demonstrating "reason"? If they cannot, then can they "compose speeches" or "carry out calculations"?

37   Freud is often criticized for "reducing normal behavior" to a kind of pathology; many say he used his theory of neurosis to criticize unfairly non-neurotic actions. Is this true in these lectures? Note that it is only on p. 183 that he mentions the psychoanalytic interest in the neuroses. Is he discussing normal and easily observed behavior or is he discussing abnormal behaviors that are especially obscure?

Lecture XII: Some Analyses of Sample Dreams

38 In this sampler of common dreams Freud notes that he cannot submit a stranger to a full interpretation since that would be a "ruthless exposure" (p. 185). Why "ruthless"? How is the concept of "resistance" connected with this dire warning?

39 If one interpretation may run to 76 pages of printed text, how can one tell when the interpretation is complete? Must there be an end to the chain of associations the dreamer brings to the task of the analysis?

40 Freud says one of his patients has an unusual ability to interpret the symbols in his own dreams (pp. 193–194). Given what we know of the mechanisms of the dream-work, what kind of characteristics might we expect to find in such a naturally talented interpreter? Would he make necessarily a good psychoanalyst?

41 Note that some elements of dream-work are absent in some of these examples (which are only parts of dream reports, after all). Dream No. 9 (p. 196) is interpretable only by way of the patient's associations. Is this true of many dreams? If so what does that mean for the use of dream interpretation techniques upon books or stories for which one has no associations?

Lecture XIII: The Archaic Features and Infantilism of Dreams

Freud introduces here for the first time an explicit reference to the ontogenetic–phylogenetic parallels he feels he has discovered with the aid of psychoanalysis. While dream interpretation is the major concern in these chapters, the implied identity between the mental life of children and that of primitives is a central feature of his critique of religion. We will see this most dramatically in *Totem and Taboo* (1912–13) and *Group Psychology* (1921).

42 "Latent thoughts do not differ from our familiar conscious thoughts of waking life" (p. 199). Why, then, are dreams so often incomprehensible to us? Why do they not yield easily to our conscious everyday efforts at understanding them? Another way to put this problem is to ask why Freud feels he has anything new to say about the interpretation of dreams.

43 On pp. 200–201 Freud speaks about his "amazement" and "astonishment" rather a lot considering how well educated he is. Why does he use these words to his audience at this juncture in the exposition? What is a "screen memory" and why does he use his personal example? Can we, his readers, gain conviction without appealing to our own experiences, e.g., of screen memories? (This is another

excellent place to sit down with a record of one's own dreams and examine them in light of Freud's claims in this chapter.)

44   People hate other people, wish them dead, are jealous of their success, and egoistic in the extreme. These facts do not surprise us, but Freud's claims about the Oedipus complex do. How does he explain the lack of gratitude the world has shown him regarding this issue?

45   About this most famous claim—that young children have strong sexual and aggressive feelings toward their caretakers—much has been written. Why might Freud have chosen the peculiar name "Oedipus" to designate this new discovery? Recall that he had earlier appealed to folklore, ordinary language (on "daydreams"), and great poets like Shakespeare and Schiller for support of his various claims. So why now Oedipus?

46   He introduces a new term—repression—and uses it to explain why dreams are so often of a sexual and aggressive quality. What is his connection between the "archaic" feelings and "unconscious" thoughts? And what is the new meaning of the word "unconscious" such that he can say "it is a particular realm of the mind" (p. 212)?

Lecture XIV: Wish-Fulfilment

This is probably the most complex chapter so far. In it Freud sets out to explain his theory, defend it against the usual criticisms, and to distinguish it from its competitors. A tall order for fifteen pages of text.

47   ". . . All dreams are children's dreams . . . , they work with the same mental impulses and mechanisms of childhood" (p. 213). Why is this so? If it is not true what happens to the argument Freud has so carefully laid out in the previous chapters?

48   Freud asks an apparently good question: "But where is wish-fulfilment, which is supposed to be the aim of the dream-work"? Yet this is a mistaken question. Why? "His [the layman's] rejection of the theory of wish-fulfilment is actually nothing other than a consequence of the dream-censorship . . ." (p. 214). Is this a fair response? (It is just this kind of point that has won Freud numerous enemies.)

49   If dreams are simply wish-fulfillments then how can there be dreams that are manifestly unpleasurable, e.g., anxiety dreams? He gives us three explanations. Compare the first against the second and third considered as a set. Is it plausible to speak of "two persons" as it were occupying a single body? Is this multiplying entities without cause, or is it following the implications of what analysis uncovers?

50   Where does the "other, censoring person" (p. 219) come from?

Can you come to Freud's rescue here, either with examples of a similar "dual personality" from literature or with reference to parapraxes? Consider the occasions upon which people plan their own "accidental" defeat. Are the subsequent punishments wish-fulfillments?

51   Note that if Freud is correct and we are able to describe a person whose wishes, when fulfilled, cause them pain, this only deepens the mystery. No? That is, if we speak of such behaviors as wish-fulfillments (which is by definition pleasurable) does that not require us to suppose that one and the same event can be both painful and pleasurable? And is this not a contradiction? It is, and it needs solving.

52   Turning to the other, more immediate battle over the universality of wish-fulfillment, Freud again speaks about two dreams. What is the difference? Recall our question about latent thoughts (No. 42 above). Are they, as unconscious thinking, restricted to archaic modes of feeling and representation?

53   ". . . All these highly complicated mental acts . . . can take place unconsciously" (p. 223). But had he not just said that dreams admit of no "no," show the most illogical of connections, etc.? The answer appears to lie in the meaning one assigns to the term "dream." What is the only proper sense we can give it?

54   To preserve the notion of wish-fulfillment Freud makes another distinction, between the "day residue" and the "archaic wish" (pp. 223–224). What is the distinction? Some dreams are especially complicated, yet all must manifest one feature, which is . . . ?

55   He is aware of how complex his exposition becomes at this point. To help clarify it he returns to the theater tickets dream. Return with him and list: (1) the latent dream-thoughts, (2) the recent wishful impulse, (3) the day residue, (4) the archaic (infantile) wish, (5) the feeling (affect) which she experienced during that day vs. the affect she had felt much earlier as a child, and (6) the means by which her displeasure was replaced by pleasure.

56   It might be good to recall the aim of dream interpretation: to undo the manifest structure that the dream-work had accomplished by way of its three modes. Why is it not adequate to note simply the archaic wish? Why not just find the infantile wish that theory tells us must lie at the base of the manifest dream?

57   Freud summarizes one of his famous analogies: that between the capitalist and entrepreneur and the unconscious wish and the day residues (p. 226). Why is he so concerned to stress that the role of capitalist and that of entrepreneur might be filled by *one* person? And why would he choose this example from economics and not from any of the other numerous occupations and professions?

(Note that if psychic determinism—one of Freud's cardinal assumptions—holds true for all persons it also holds true for Freud and his choice of examples.)

Lecture XV: Uncertainties and Criticisms

As he promised, Freud is more than willing both to point out what appear to be gaps in his theory and to list unexplained facts. He arranges them in four sets.

58 In the first he raises questions about the arbitrariness of interpretations. Are these valid points? What other endeavors in the sciences or the humanities rely upon "skillful interpreters"? It is not accidental that he returns to the theme of archaic languages, e.g., Egyptian hieroglyphic script as well as cuneiform writing. Is this a valid example? (See the recent essays on the problem of interpretation noted in the appendixes.) Why does the "system of expression" of dream thoughts occupy a less favorable position than these other ancient scripts?

59 How might one conduct an experiment on dream interpretation similar to the experiment conducted by the Royal Asiatic Society in 1857? Which of the two experiments would be the easier to perform? Note that Freud sometimes speaks about translating the manifest dream back into its latent dream thoughts and into the archaic wish that "fueled" it. Why is the word "translation" an unfortunate term to use here?

60 Another set of objections to Freud is that psychoanalytic theory and interpretations are farfetched and extraordinary. Is this a severe problem? Why would Freud use the frontier control example in his response to these objections (recall his earlier images of judge and criminals)? Dreams are often constructed like a joke: but why do they leave us cold (p. 236)?

61 A more vexing problem now emerges: some of his students and colleagues reject his major thesis. How does he explain their disagreement? Furthermore, does the existence of a number of contrary theories argue against the plausibility of each? Is this a principle one can apply to other scientific claims?

62 How does his distinction between the dream material and the dream itself disarm this fourth objection to his theory? Is it a plausible defense? If two people report the same manifest content, induced by hypnotic suggestion, does that mean that both people must have produced the dream using the same method and that each dream means the same thing to each dreamer? If I dream of my father dying and you dream of your father dying, do the two dreams mean the same thing? To both of us alike?

The last sentence of this chapter outlines the road Freud will follow as he passes from the investigation of harmless parapraxes to the analysis of normal dreams to the explanation of the sufferings of neurotics. It is also a hint at the grandeur of his conception when he notes the "rapidity of the transformation which makes a dreamer into a waking and reasonable man." It is just such a transformation that psychoanalytic therapy aims to effect with the neurotic whose waking life is dominated by unexamined dreams.

PART THREE

Lecture XVI: Psycho-Analysis and Psychiatry

The remaining thirteen lectures differ greatly from the first fifteen. In the first half Freud treated his audience and readers as co-investigators, often giving them the better lines, and always appealing to their own experience and reason. This changes to a much more didactic mode. Yet it is hardly less fascinating. For here we see Freud at his strength as he first sketches out portraits of human beings in torment and then grapples with the task of explaining their sufferings.

These chapters also afford us a more direct view of Freud's own character, a phenomenon that some cherish as an exemplar of truthfulness and others reject as overweening and prideful. The text and the man will speak for themselves.

1   Why is benevolent skepticism the most desirable attitude for both critics and patients of psychoanalysis to manifest? Do these lectures foster this kind of attitude?

2   Freud immediately describes part of his usual working day, including a description of the famous double doors. Is it customary for a host to point out that his or her guest has made an error upon entering the room? Even after he has embarrassed some poor person who cannot shut the door, Freud persists in remarking upon such errors? Is this an example of hauteur on a grand scale? Why does Freud persist?

3   He goes on to say that many of these patients are disrespectful and arrogant. Is this fair? Note that Freud is perfectly sincere in these comments about his patients. Is that sincerity a necessary part of the treatment?

4   A brief case history follows. Like the detective or judge whose profession is to ferret out the true account from the brambles of the false, Freud pays special attention to the way in which the story is told. Why would "gaps" in the account be of particular interest? Or why should we be especially sensitive to words like "incredible," "suddenly," and phrases like "as if by magic"?

5   Freud contrasts his method with that of the traditional psychia-
     trist (pp. 254–255). Is this a fair comparison? Note that questions
     like those he raises on p. 253 are essential to his work. Is this sim-
     ply part of his teaching style? What other professions rely upon
     this kind of question—other than judges and the police? Would
     standard medical education be the best means for training people
     to become adept at this kind of questioning?

6   Is psychoanalysis primarily a mode of treatment? Note that Freud is
     overly modest, for by 1916, the year in which he delivered these
     lectures, he could count numerous cases of outright cure. So why
     does he stress the powerlessness of his method to remove symptoms?

Lecture XVII: The Sense of Symptoms

7   After crediting three other men with the discovery that neurotic
     symptoms have a hidden meaning, Freud describes the two forms
     of neurosis with which he is most concerned. Compare the two.
     Why, again, are the silly, irrational, and crazy features of these
     diseases especially pertinent to psychoanalytic inquiry?

8   Contrary to what he said (above, question 6), he here reports two
     dramatic cures: the first a spontaneous recovery of the meaning of
     an obsession; the second the result of many hours of treatment.
     When does the first occur (p. 261)? Note the metaphors Freud
     uses to describe the structure of her illness: are these typical of
     most scientific accounts?

9   Reading these short descriptions may appear to be a mild chore
     compared to reading the detailed theoretical sections of Freud's
     essays on dreams and other technical subjects. Why is this an
     incorrect assessment? Why can one not simply skim these case
     histories and proceed to the real issue, the theory?

10   If a patient does not receive relief from his symptoms does that
     mean that the proffered interpretations were incorrect? In other
     words, can one imagine a case in which a person recognized the
     "truth" of the explanation put forth but persisted in the neurotic
     behavior?

Lecture XVIII: Fixation to Trauma—The Unconscious

11   Why does Freud use the term "economic" when he gives an
     account of the traumatic illnesses (p. 275)? After introducing it as
     a plausible concept that will permit us to explain both war
     neuroses and hysteria, he puts it aside. Why?

12   "Mental processes had therefore been at work in her . . ." (p. 277).
     How does Freud move from this observation to his grander claim
     that there is an unconscious mental process? What features of her

"crazy" actions permit us to say they are products of a mind—
rather than merely accidental occurrences?

13   There was and is no lack of philosophers and rational thinkers
willing to prove that there can be no unconscious mind. Why is
Freud not grateful for their guidance?

14   "The construction of a symptom is a substitute for something else
that did not happen" (p. 280). If this is true what is the task of psychotherapy? Upon discovering the likely meaning of a symptom
why cannot the psychoanalyst simply tell the patient these truths
and so undo the neurosis? Note that Freud returns to the theme of
"work" (p. 281). Is "work" a dynamic or an economic concept?

15   Freud is one of the most widely cited authors of this century—his
name appears in an immense variety of scholarly and non-scholarly
works. Yet he is also one of the most widely abused authors (a frequent criticism being that he is authoritarian and dogmatic in his
pronouncements about the infallibility of psychoanalysis). Is this
true of this chapter? If not how can you explain the particular vehemence which his name still evokes?

Lecture XIX: Resistance and Repression

16   Freud had used the term "economic" to describe the traumatic
neuroses. How is that term related to the two central "observations"
in this chapter? Why is the existence of resistance a "strange fact"
(p. 286)?

17   Resistance would appear to occur in the analysis of all persons—
even the well-educated. Why are they not immune from this
characteristic? Why does Freud refuse to grant "sanctuary" to his
patients who wish to keep some things secret?

18   Why do otherwise intelligent people act like emotional imbeciles
(p. 293) whenever the analysis touches upon a topic that is near to
their "unconscious conflict"? Is the vehemence and stridency of a
patient's objections to the analysis a sign of the therapist's failure
or something else? Which is primary, the "critical faculty" or the
set of emotional attitudes? Given Freud's answer, what is the
likelihood of a person's completing a successful self-analysis?

19   On pp. 294–298 Freud suggests a series of theoretical models of
the behaviors he has described, e.g., the two rooms (a public one
and a private one) connected by a door at which a watchman
prevents certain guests from entering into the public domain.
Freud is aware that there are no little men (or women) who live
in our brains; why does he, then, pursue this analogy with the
watchman? Why must this model account for normal psychology
as well as that of neurotics (p. 297)?

20   He introduces the technical term "transference neuroses" and then
      a special use of the term "frustration" (p. 300). How does the
      latter term prefigure his comments on the social basis of the
      neuroses? The watchman, he says, "represses" certain thoughts
      and does not permit them public exposure. How is this related to
      the activities of the dream censor? Yet, he concludes, symptoms
      are "compromise formations"—they accomplish, or attempt to
      accomplish, two distinct objectives at one and the same time. Are
      these objectives ever compatible with one another? In which
      "realm" or part of the mind can one find both an intention and its
      opposite flourishing side by side? And in which normal behaviors?

Lectures XX–XXIII:
Sexuality and Human Development

Technical Terms

Libido; sexual object; sexual aim; latency; polymorphously perverse;
erotogenic zones; autoeroticism; defence; sadism; inhibition; Oedipus
complex; pregenital trends; regression; cathexis; component instincts;
organ-pleasure; love object; ambivalence; sublimation; adhesiveness of
the libido; repression

Lecture XX: The Sexual Life of Human Beings

21   Freud begins his comments on the term "sexual" with a joking refer-
      ence to learned experts. Why? And why is he willing to forgo offer-
      ing a strict and exact definition of the term before venturing into his
      descriptions? Is the element of "secrecy" an unimportant feature of
      his or our understanding of sexuality? Note that Freud feels no com-
      punctions about using the terms pervert and perversion. Is this true
      of contemporary psychiatry?
22   Clarify the distinction between sexual object and sexual aim
      (p. 305). On what grounds does Freud compare these types of sexual
      activities with "normal" heterosexual, adult intercourse? Why is the
      presence of "excessive sacrifices" a sign of sexuality (p. 306)?
23   ". . . Homosexual impulses are invariably discovered in every sin-
      gle neurotic . . ." (p. 307). How does Freud's general thesis about
      the sexuality of children help us account for this clinical claim?
      How does that same thesis allow him to explain why the depriva-
      tion of normal sexual satisfaction "brings out perverse inclinations
      in people" (p. 310)? Define "polymorphously perverse." Of whom
      is it descriptive?
24   Freud is aware that his thoughts on children will not pass uncrit-
      icized by the majority of official spokespersons. Yet he turns the

tables on his critics, one of his accomplished skills, by pointing out the source of their hostile rejection (pp. 311–312). Is this fair? How does his retort fit into his larger claims about the nature of civilization itself?

25 He goes on to catalogue a variety of "sexual" behaviors in which, he says, all infants and children engage. How does he link these innocent childish activities with those of adult perverts? Indeed, he says if children have any kind of sexual life it must be perverse. Why? What other sources of confirmation or illustration might he turn to for additional support? Why are children given a "depreciatory and incomplete explanation" of sex? Is this true of our contemporary life too? Why is education, say in school classes, about sexuality incapable of preventing the development of both repression and symptoms? Is this a pessimistic conclusion?

Lecture XXI: The Development of the Libido and the Sexual Organizations

This is a crucial lecture. In it Freud outlines his major claims about the nature of both infantile sexuality and the core-complex that appears to underlie many neurotic conditions: the Oedipus complex.

26 In other contexts he speaks of the principle of the psychic unity of mankind. Why would he be so concerned to promote this principle? How does he demonstrate that normal infants, outright perverts, neurotics, and normal adults, as well as great poets all manifest "perverse" tendencies? Why is he so adamant about calling these things sexual when the term "organ-pleasure" appears to be less theoretically biased (p. 323)?

27 He then calls up an analogy. He compares the development of the apple tree and the bean from seedlings that appear identical with the development of overt sexual pleasures (including perverse sexual pleasures) from infantile behaviors (pp. 324–325). For this analogy to hold, what must he believe about the sources of infantile "sexuality"?

28 In a somewhat roundabout fashion he describes four major phases of infantile and childhood sexuality: oral, anal, a period of latency, and the efflorescence of adolescence. Why is it important to underscore the events that occur just prior to latency (p. 326)? To what does the term "infantile repression" refer?

29 Contrary to what one might expect, he does not say that the pregenital instincts are a unified set of impulses that one can see operate, as it were, in a coherent and consistent manner. Rather there are "breaks" (p. 328) in the development of the libido: where else has he drawn our attention to the existence of breaks or gaps?

30 How does the multiplicity of pregenital instincts compare to the number of potential targets (objects) of those instincts? And when does the number of objects decrease, such that, in normal children, one finds that only a single person (object) remains as the target for their affections? (Cf. "the psychical work of repression" on p. 329.)

31 This leads us to consider the Oedipus complex—a term of far-reaching significance in his thinking. After calling upon the authority of Sophocles Freud says that the latter's play, which is replete with illicit sexuality, the murder of a father, and mutilation, never incites condemnation. Yet his (Freud's) work does. Why? Why would one text gain an immense stature, especially within cultivated circles, and another, dealing with precisely the same topic, receive so much rancorous abuse?

32 If Sophocles, and even Goethe, the great German poet, spoke about oedipal feelings in children before him, why does Freud claim that his theory is revolutionary? Another way of raising this question is: Why was it only in Freud's work that these bits of wisdom from past sages gained a central place in a psychological theory? Given Freud's understanding of the nature of social constraints and the reality of repression, can one say that the former are symptoms while the latter, psychoanalytic science, is the cure?

33 The standard criticism raised against Freud's theory about the source of incest taboos is that they have a biological not a psychological foundation. As animal breeders know, mixing blood lines too closely can create genetically inferior stock. Yet Freud says the very existence of incest taboos and other such rules indicates that the constraints upon incest are not genetically based. Is this reasonable? What kinds of behavior are legally constrained within this society? On the other hand, what kinds of behavior are encouraged in sermons, lectures and other official organs of wisdom?

34 With the advent of puberty children must confront again the issues dealt with by repression just prior to latency. Why? That is, why did these issues and the infantile wishes associated with them not fade away, like most memories from childhood? He uses the term "cathected" with libido (p. 336, n. 2). What has persisted, then, the "energy" attached to an infantile urge or the urge itself?

35 Does the evidence from dream interpretation support or weaken Freud's claim about the universality of oedipal feelings? If the former what can we conclude about the "archaic source" of the dream wish? Is psychoanalysis primarily a theory about certain rare forms of mental disease called neurosis or something else? It would pay us to underline the last sentence in this chapter (p. 338). If Freud is correct, can ordinary people use psychoanalytic

principles to investigate the "depth structure" of their own dreams or of cultural artifacts, like novels and plays? What inner constraints might prevent one from achieving a full understanding of the unconscious themes in one's own life or in artistic products?

Lecture XXII: Some Thoughts on Development and Regression–Aetiology

36 In order to explain the difference between "fixation" (of an instinct) and "regression" (back to an earlier libidinal mode), Freud uses a number of analogies. Which is the best? (Note that there are many distinct instincts or "libidinal tendencies," not just one that develops over time.)

37 How can the investigation of adult neurotic patients cast any light on the normal developmental process (p. 341)? This is no small claim, for if correct it means that psychoanalytic investigations are one way to recover the otherwise inobservable sequences that go to make up the complex institution called adult sexual behavior. Is this institution a singular or composite structure? At what other junctures can one see some of the parts of which it is composed?

38 He briefly discusses the difference between "repression" and "regression" (p. 343). Which is typical of hysteria, and which of obsessional neurosis? What on earth could "sadistic-anal-organization" mean? He has not prepared us for this unique term, and it will make little sense to us until we have read his "Rat Man" case history (below, "Notes Upon a Case of Obsessional Neurosis," 1909).

39 There is one key sentence : "A regression of the libido without repression would never produce a neurosis but would lead to a perversion" (p. 344). If this is true what then is the structural relationship between perversions and the neuroses? That is, if the existence of perversion means that repression has not occurred, are there any "symptoms" that will be amenable to psychoanalytic treatment? If not, what can we conclude about the value of psychoanalysis for treating such "disorders"?

40 He then addresses the murky issue of the aetiology of the neuroses. Why can there be no single agent or source responsible for the generation of a neurotic condition, e.g., a trauma? Consider his metaphors on p. 345—about the sexual impulses and their "intercommunicating channels." Why would he find this image—which will reappear in many of his essays—especially attractive?

41 "Sublimation" is one of the more vexatious concepts in Freud's thought. Try to explain what he means here when he says it "consists in the sexual trend abandoning its aim of obtaining a component or

a reproductive pleasure and taking on another which is related genetically to the abandoned one but is itself no longer sexual and must be described as social" (p. 345). Of which kind of sexual trends (or part instincts, or libidinal currents) can this be true? Can the fully mature genital organization abandon the aim of heterosexual intercourse?

42   An illustration or two of "sublimation" would be immensely helpful; unfortunately Freud offers us none. Given the little we know thus far about the pregenital libidinal trends, e.g., oral and anal sexuality, what can we say of their "aims" and "pleasures"? Can sublimation—a term derived from alchemy, by the way—ever work for the whole of sexuality? Is sublimation akin to the "sublime" that poets and religious authorities often speak of?

43   How does the concept of "complemental series" help Freud account for his lack of success both in predicting which people will become neurotic, and, explaining why they and not their siblings, for example, became his patients? Compare prediction and postdiction in other sciences or modes of investigation. Can literary critics predict the content of an author's next book? Or can they predict which young writer will become a great author and of those that are great, look back into their past and show the clear lines of development that lead from their earliest efforts to their present success?

44   After noting how libidinal choices are of an "adhesive" nature, Freud distinguishes between external and internal frustrations which, according to the theory, together produce a neurotic condition. Why does he add that internal frustrations themselves may have been external at one time? What time was that?

45   What are the "ego instincts" (pp. 350–351) and why do popular accounts of psychoanalysis, and more so, critics of psychoanalysis overlook them? Why did the first psychoanalysts investigate the sexual instincts rather than the instincts associated with the ego? Can a neurotic condition exist without the active conflict of ego instincts with sexual ones? Must treatment focus, therefore, upon the analysis of both sets of instincts?

46   To illustrate his distinctions he makes up a story about two little girls. Why does he assign the burden of neurosis to the middle-class girl and not her proletarian playmate? When Freud says the neurotic had a "higher moral and intellectual development," is he being ironic or honest?

47   He then takes up a point of view we have not yet seen: namely, metaphysics. Must one agree with these latter remarks if one has agreed with him so far? Why are the "sexual instincts" harder to educate than the ego instincts? Which set of instincts is most typically addressed by either legislation or morality?

48 What is his evidence for his grand claim that pleasure is "in some way connected with the diminution, reduction or extinction of the amounts of stimulus prevailing in the mental apparatus" (p. 356)? What is a "mental apparatus"? How might one verify his claim about the supremacy of the sexual act? Would other philosophical systems or religious institutions support this kind of claim? Why or why not?

Lecture XXIII: The Paths to the Formation of Symptoms

This is the most compact and the most abstract lecture of the group. Where before Freud gave us a few examples to enliven the presentation and ease us along, here he elaborates his central theory of the source of hysterical symptoms in a way that cannot be bettered, nor further condensed. As we will see in the lecture following this one, he is aware of these special difficulties.

49 First, Freud defines the term "symptoms" (p. 358). What is the key to ascertaining whether or not a patient has a particular symptom? Are symptoms the same as signs or indicators? Can psychoanalytic treatment work if the patient has no complaints, no problems, and no discomfort? If there is no discomfort what must the therapist bring about before the work of treatment can begin?

50 He sometimes calls symptoms compromise formations. What other physical product might be termed the product of a compromise between two, distinct, parts of the mind? How does the fixation "lure" the libido into the path of regression (p. 359)? Why does he use the verb "lured" here?

51 "The ideas to which it now transfers its energy as a cathexis belong to the system of the unconscious and are subject to the processes there, particularly to condensation and displacement" (p. 359). If this is so, to which aspect of the process of dream formation do the original libidinal aims correspond? In other words, why do we find that neurotics cannot express their repressed libidinal aims? And why do we find that their symptoms—the compulsions, fears, and other ailments of which they complain— are themselves complicated and often unintelligible, except upon arduous analysis?

52 What factors contribute to the formation of the symptom so that it "emerges" as a "many-times distorted derivative of the unconscious libidinal wish-fulfilment, an ingeniously chosen piece of ambiguity with two meanings in complete mutual contradiction" (p. 360)? The manifest dream is produced, he says, in a similar way except it is less distorted and has fewer absolute negations

obvious within it. Why is the dream less dangerous for the dreamer than the libidinal trend is for the neurotic who is wide awake?

53   Recall Freud's earlier discussion of the archaic elements in dreams (Lecture XIII, above): How many types of archaicisms does he describe in this lecture? Is his notion of a "prehistoric" experience necessary to the exposition of his theory of the genesis of hysteria? (Is his model of evolution Darwinian or Lamarckian?) Does he rule out a genetic explanation for the onset of neurotic conditions?

54   Why must all neurotics deny any validity to an initial psychoanalytic investigation of their symptoms? Is Freud being ironic when he says we can disregard a patient's (accurate) claim that he or she has no access to or any recognition of the truths which the analysis of a particular symptom has brought about? If a person knew exactly what his/her behavior meant would he be a patient at all? Would he/she be a neurotic?

55   Freud prides himself on his honesty, perhaps with good reason, for he adds another level of complexity to his exposition when he notes that having investigated the infantile precursors of symptoms we find they are sometimes merely fantasies. (Note that the English translator uses English spellings; we will use American except in direct quotations.) Some patients recall accurately that they were seduced by older children; other patients have exactly the same recollection but it is false. Does this remove psychoanalysis from among the set of plausible theories about human behavior?

56   As is his wont, when faced with a conundrum of this sort he proffers a distinction: this time between psychical and material reality (pp. 369–370). Why is it proper to say that the former kind may be a throwback to an even earlier material sort?

57   Also as is his wont he asks an excellent question: "How does the libido find its way [back] to these points of fixation" (p. 373)? What does the "hypercathexis of phantasies" (p. 374) mean? If the "quantitative factor" is a major element in the aetiology of a neurotic symptom, can we use it to predict—roughly—when a person is most likely to exhibit neurotic behavior? For example? (Note his earlier discussion of adolescence and the term "dementia praecox".)

58   How does the quantitative factor work in the case of artists? Why do they have more at their disposal? Given this interpretation would you predict that artists would welcome or decline the chance to enter into psychoanalytic treatment? Recall Freud's earlier discussion of Sophocles—a great artist, surely—and the special pleasures his plays continue to afford audiences. In what does their special charm lie? Will you expect to find that case

histories are also charming and fascinating in the manner of a play or novel? (Recall the "bad jokes" in dreams above.)

Lecture XXIV: The Common Neurotic State

In this rather chatty lecture, which is misleadingly titled since it has little to do with "our" common neurotic state, Freud makes a number of apparently routine comments. Yet they are of profound importance for us since they are basic to his understanding of what makes psychoanalysis a unique science.

59 He correctly identifies his reader's state of mind having just finished the former lecture with its abstract descriptions. Yet he obstinately refuses to apologize. Why? Why not begin his exposition with more sensational stories from the annals of the field?

60 Many schools of philosophy and depth psychology developed, in part, as responses to psychoanalysis. Most of their practitioners begin treatment with an examination of the patient's point of view: for example, they would ask Dora how she understood the meaning of her symptoms. "Phenomenological" psychology requires the therapist to examine closely the particular conscious meanings a patient assigns to his or her experiences. Why does Freud reject this apparently sensible and fair route to understanding the meaning of a symptom?

61 He then uses a theatrical analogy to describe the varieties of possible neurotic forms with which the psychoanalyst must be concerned. Recall his earlier analogies: Why is he so keen on these social or group comparisons? Why are traumatic neuroses—which have actual and often violent origins—not a problem of his theory of the aetiology of symptoms?

62 Explain "flight into illness," "secondary function," and "secondary gain" (pp. 383–384). Why, according to Freud, does the existence of the latter, in which the neurosis appears to aid the patient, not count for much? Is this a value judgment or a clinical one? Why is it better to go down in an honorable struggle?

63 He attempts to distinguish between two great classes of neuroses: the "actual neuroses" and "psychoneuroses" (pp. 386–387). Can his theory account for both types? Are both types amenable to strictly psychoanalytic treatment? Must every patient manifest only one type or the other?

64 Is psychoanalysis a complete science? To which fields must it look for its ultimate grounding and verification? Why is Freud so concerned with the notion of sexual noxa? Yet, at that time, what characterized psychoanalytic research? Would medical training be a necessity for that kind of work?

65 Sometimes the "actual neurosis" gives rise to a "psycho-neurosis" (pp. 390–391). How? And how could one tell when that shift had occurred?

Lecture XXV: Anxiety

66 Anxiety would appear to be one of those topics about which everyone has direct knowledge—yet Freud says we are not sufficiently surprised that neurotics suffer from it especially. Why? And why does he reject the anatomical study of anxiety, or any other emotion?

67 He offers a minimal distinction between normal and pathological anxiety and then leaps back to a biological theory: Is his distinction plausible? Why does the prehistory of the species question arise here? Must one accept both these biological speculations if one has agreed up to this point with his other claims about neurosis and dreams?

68 What distinguishes the three types of anxiety? The third type—a grown man afraid to cross a street—seems the most irrational. Why does that make them the most amenable to psychoanalytic investigation? (The SE editor points out that Freud's theory of anxiety went through a number of changes; what we see here is only one small segment of that larger discussion.)

69 Some kinds of anxiety, he says, are simply the products of an increase in sexual tension (pp. 401–402). But that of hysterics, especially, is not directly tied to sexual frustrations. How does the notion of "secondary revision" (taken from dream theory) help him explain the puzzling diversity of phobias found in the analysis of hysteric patients?

70 Finally, he attempts to link his discussion of symptoms with the analysis of anxiety (p. 404). How does repression figure into the generation of anxiety, and, in turn, how do we know that neurotic symptoms "are only formed to escape an otherwise unavoidable generating of anxiety" (p. 404)?

71 What is the ego's role in the generation of both "realistic" and neurotic anxiety? Flight or fight are the two great defensive operations open to all creatures in the face of imminent danger. These are active behaviors in response to external dangers. What are their psychical counterparts? (See also p. 420.)

72 What does "bound anxiety" mean and to what is it contrasted? Can it serve the entire set of needs of the individual? Recall Freud's discussion of anxiety dreams—does their existence pose a problem for his general theory of wish-fulfillment? If not, can he use a similar line of argument regarding the anxiety produced by

neurotic fantasies? (The case histories discussed below will give us a much better description of anxiety and its alleviation.)

73 Consider the beautiful story on p. 407 about the child in the dark room. Why would the child's longing—experienced in the dark—be transformed into a fear of the dark? That is, why, according to the theory outlined above, would the ego transform an emotional (intrapsychic) need into a phobia of an external thing? Which kind of anxiety—real or neurotic—appears first in the development of most children? Why would earlier emotional traumas have more severe impact than later ones?

74 How does repression contribute to the generation of "bound anxieties"? What are the "two phases of the neurotic process" (p. 410)? Given his account of the "fortress," why would the ego have to erect a continuous series of symptoms? That is, can Freud now explain why neurotics are driven to repeat behaviors that are obviously unpleasant and often self-destructive?

75 Consider your own anxiety dreams—if you cannot recall one consider an account of that of another person. Are the objects that terrify you in the dream terrifying in reality? Or is there a mix? Are they sometimes like grizzly bears? And at other times, are they frightening only during the dream? How could Freud account for the latter?

Lecture XXVI: The Libido Theory and Narcissism

As he observes midway through this lecture he is far less clear about the nature of "narcissism" than he is about the three neuroses—hysteria, obsessive-compulsive, and anxiety—which he had studied since the late 1890s, a period of more than twenty years. This lecture requires, therefore, careful reading. One must struggle to distinguish outright speculations from clinical observations, and both of these from comments upon methodology.

76 Perhaps the most perplexing, as well as the most typical, quality of Freud's presentation is his insistence upon retaining a complex account in face of a more attractive, if simpler, grand theory. Why, in other words, does he not accept Jung's suggestion that it would be more elegant to speak not of two sets of instincts (ego and sexual), but one? Why not suppose there is but one form of psychic energy that could assume many guises, like physical energy that may appear as heat or potential energy or other forms of a single kind of energy, all of which are transformable into one another?

77 Freud's candor immediately costs us some hard won clarity when he first distinguishes between "sexual instincts" and "self-preservative

instincts" (p. 414) but then speaks about "narcissism," which entails a notion of sexualized ego instincts (or ego-libido). How does he use Abraham's theory of dementia praecox (what is now termed schizophrenia) to account for the sexualized cathexis of the ego (p. 415)? (Note the weight Freud gives to the observation that these schizophrenic patients over-value their bodies.)

78   He immediately refers back to a theory of sleep and dreaming. Why is sleep so attractive to him as a model of the "primal state of the distribution of the libido" (p. 417)? Which, according to this account, is first—ego-interests or object-libido? Consider his analogy of the amoeba (p. 416) and its use of pseudopodia: does it permit him to "explain" or "describe" complex functioning? (What is the difference between the two?)

79   What is the tell-tale sign that a person, say a young man, has expended some of his own narcissism upon another person? (Note that the topic of narcissism is of central importance in Freud: the SE editor points out the major texts.) Will this sign be present also in other instances where one expends or transfers narcissistic cathexis onto another person or thing? For example?

80   The Goethe poem, unfortunately presented in a nearly unintelligible translation, is to illustrate sexual overvaluation. Explain the line, "I to my very self am lost" (p. 418). Given the complexity of this topic it would help to have more examples of this kind of overvaluation—especially since it will play a decisive role in Freud's critique of religion.

81   Explicate the two critical questions Freud places in his listeners' mouths (p. 420). He says everyone withdraws their object libido during sleep, and then, upon awakening, sends it back (p. 421). Is this a plausible generalization? What kind of everyday behaviors illustrate this reversal?

82   He suggests that our knowledge of regression and fixation in transference neurotics (transference being a term which he will not explain until the next lecture) may help us account for the genesis of schizophrenic symptoms. How?

83   We then read a most obscure paragraph about restitution and the shadow of objects (p. 422). The SE editor refers us to two of Freud's theoretical papers. Yet can we piece together what Freud is saying here—if we follow out the metaphor of the thing and its shadow? Schizophrenics, according to this account, mistake the shadow or image or an idea of a thing for the thing itself. During what daily period do normal people engage in precisely the same error? And with what results?

84   There is no lack of self-conscious reflections by philosophers and other learned people about their conscious experiences, their

ideas, and their perceptions. Why does Freud reject these sources of information? (Ricoeur, a contemporary philosopher, has called Freud an "anti-phenomenologist"—why might he have written this?)

85 Although psychoanalysts had not, at that time, studied schizophrenia as intensely as they had investigated the classical neuroses, Freud makes some comments about the genesis of some symptoms, especially paranoid delusions of persecution (pp. 424–427). Granted that he is correct about these particular cases, would it follow that the same kind of conflicts would engender paranoid delusions in our time? Would a change in sexual mores bring about a change in the structure of unconscious processes? For example? Would paranoid symptoms vary from time to time and place to place therefore?

86 The study of narcissistic disorders (among which Freud is now including many types of schizophrenia) led him to recognize a split in the internal structure of the ego. He calls part of this split an "ideal ego" (p. 429). (It is intimately tied to his later, more famous, notion of the superego. The superego, in turn, is a central concept in his analysis of religion.) What provides the ideal ego its energy? And what determines its shape?

87 Freud cannot resist adding an afterthought—another sign that this is not a systematic presentation of deduced truths—about the source of anxiety in the presence of danger (p. 430). He attempts to distinguish between a behavior—running away from danger— and one's conscious feelings—fear. On what grounds? That is, with what principle taken from what field of inquiry, does he make this distinction?

Lecture XXVII: Transference

88 Though a little late in coming, Freud now offers to explain what this central term means. This and the final chapter are the only ones devoted to the technique of psychoanalytic therapy—surely a fascinating subject to his listeners. Why does he place them, therefore, at the end of his exposition of the essentials of his science?

89 Is he on the side of "civilized sexual morality" or of its opposite, a kind of hedonism of which there were no lack of examples even in his day? What degree of persuasive power does he ascribe to the therapist (or any other person) relative to the two forces which contend with one another and which create neurotic symptoms? How does therapy help the polar bear and the whale meet on the same ground (p. 433)?

90 Why are cures by persuasion, change of habit, exhortation, and

religious transformation, not compatible with cure brought about through analysis? He offers one of his many famous formulas on p. 435 when he describes the task of his kind of therapy. Which of the numerous concepts discussed above is essential to his formula? Will psychoanalysis as a treatment work with outright perverts? (See above, question no. 21.)

91   Does Freud believe his method is the final and authoritative means of bringing about therapeutic change? Why is it not a causal method of cure? Regarding Freud's alleged dogmatism about the validity of his science, is it in evidence here in this chapter? How does repression operate in patients such that no amount of "education" will suffice to replace their unconscious thoughts? Does the answer to this question also help explain why simply reading Freud himself is not sufficient to the task of solving one's own difficulties?

92   But it sometimes works—with which type of patients? What psychological characteristic do persons suffering from hysteria, or obsessional neurosis, or anxiety neurosis share? Recalling his last lecture what psychological characteristic do the patients listed on pp. 438–439 share? Given his description of the development of libidinal positions in chapter XXVI, is it fair to say that in this period of his thought he does not believe psychoanalytic therapy is feasible for persons suffering from pre-oedipal fixations or regressions? Is it worthwhile for analysts to investigate such conditions?

93   Now he describes the transference proper (pp. 439ff.). Is it a rare event brought about only by the esoteric workings of the analytic process in the secrecy and gloom of the consulting room? Why does he say a person with sharper eyes will confess with no hesitation that a patient's glowing reports of the therapist's genius are really quite boring? What factors guarantee that such glowing reports must be boring to reasonable people?

94   Might the therapist experience a modicum of boredom as well at this incessant flow of praise and glory? You have no doubt observed Freud's wry sense of humor, including humor about himself and his profession. What functions might this kind of humor serve? That is, how might it help the therapist guard against dancing to the patient's tune? In what other professions or in what similar circumstances do you find a wry sense of humor to be a typical characteristic?

95   If transference is an ordinary thing, observed in numerous relationships, why does Freud count it as an unexpected novelty (p. 439)? Why does it constitute a formidable resistance to the treatment? While the more observant friends of a patient may detect a bit too much repetition in the latter's praises (or attacks)

upon the good doctor, what is the patient's understanding of these feelings? Are they distinguishable from any similar feelings he or she may have had at other times about other people?

96 If patients cannot, initially, distinguish transference feelings from other, similarly intense, feelings, how valid are such self-reports? That is, if transference occurs regularly in the analysis of certain kinds of neurotics, to which factors—patient self-understandings or patient behaviors—must the therapist attach most significance?

97 Freud says there are two modes transference may manifest: a positive one and a negative one (p. 443). Is either a better sign than the other of the patient's chances at eventual recovery? Do good people show positive feelings and bad people negative feelings about the therapist? Why would the negative aspects of the transference appear later in the treatment than the positive aspects which appear from the beginning? Does the treatment create or fabricate the negative features of the transference?

98 How is it that the therapy comes to focus upon an artificial neurosis rather than upon the original problems that brought the patient into treatment? Why are hysteria, obsessional neurosis and anxiety neurosis (also termed anxiety hysteria) rightly termed "transference neuroses"? What features do they share such that Freud says one cannot doubt his basic claims as to their libidinal character?

99 He concludes his lecture by arguing or demonstrating that psychoanalytic treatment cannot be applied to persons who exhibit a narcissistic neurosis (a vague term, since he had previously spoken of narcissistic forms of psychosis, a much more severe malady). Do they manifest in their behavior the conflicts typical of repressed wishes? What universal characteristic do they lack such that Freud excludes them from among the group of people who might benefit from psychoanalytic therapy? What kinds of feelings and behavior must they exhibit before we could be reasonably sure that psychoanalysis would help them?

Lecture XXVIII: Analytic Therapy

In this final lecture Freud simply outlines the basic features of his method of therapy. As Freud readily admits it is not an adequate account of the many subtle elements and technical considerations that operate in the conduct of an actual case. (To see those more clearly we turn to his extensive case histories in the next section.) Yet it effectively summarizes many key elements of the preceding lectures.

100 He began his psychiatric practice using suggestion, a method which required him to hypnotize his patient, through a variety of means, and then to "force" the symptom to depart. Often this

required him to touch his patient, pressing this, now that part of the patient's body. Why might this latter technique have contributed to the more spectacular of sudden cures?

101 He returns, again, to the notion of "work" on p. 450 when he describes the ease with which suggestion effected cures. How does he link the theoretical concept "work" (in all the ways that term is used in these lectures) with the equally theoretical term "energy"? Why is analysis the inverse of hypnosis?

102 Is free association, a task he assigns both to the interpretation of dreams and to the interpretation of symptoms, an easy skill to acquire? Or does it demand work? (Recall his list of excuses, complaints, maladies, and other responses people bring to the job of remembering their dreams, and of verbalizing or recording their free associations, without censoring them as either too trivial or too disgusting.) Why is "lifting internal resistances" serious work (p. 451)?

103 While analysis is more than suggestion, it does not exclude suggestion from among its tools of forcing the patient to give up an earlier libidinal position. Where and how ought it to be employed? Perhaps psychoanalytic patients manifest typical sexual themes because their physician, their therapist imposes them, via suggestion, upon the treatment? If so, perhaps then we will find that another theoretical orientation, one which rejects the libido theory, produces an analysis with no sexual themes whatsoever. How does Freud answer both these challenges?

104 Pages 454–455 contain a concise formulation about the dynamics of cure—according to the libido theory. If therapy works because it permits the patient's ego to avoid a fresh repression, and if repression is an automatic response to the threat of anxiety, what emotional state must the patient pass through, at least initially, following the removal of these repressive barriers? In other words, are all the difficulties and fears that beset the neurotic products of irrational thoughts which upon enlightenment will vanish from view and cease operating?

105 A popular understanding of transference is that it is simply a reenactment, in the present, of a prior relationship that somehow went wrong. Hence, according to this view, transference responses are historical repetitions. Does Freud support this view? Why is he so fond of using metaphors drawn from warfare to describe the events of therapy? (Note that the original German term for cathexis, "Besetzung" [occupation], refers to the activity foreign troops engage in when they occupy an enemy territory.)

106 Returning to his first subject, Freud notes that the dreams of normal people do not differ significantly from either the dreams or

the symptoms of neurotics. Why does he stress this point? Why is it a mistake to say that the dreams of normals are distorted and symptom-like in their structure only because they are the products of a sleepy mental mechanism that cannot process adequately an otherwise coherent and unconflicted message?

107   Freud next lists a number of reasons for therapeutic failures. He blames errors in training, crudity of technique, mis-diagnoses, and other aspects of the therapist's behavior. Yet he also blames the patient's family. Is this fair? Do not all parents or spouses wish for their loved one's full and complete recovery at the earliest possible moment? (Cf. his comment about settling a family's estate.)

108   If Freud's initial observations on the genesis of parapraxes, on the interpretation of dreams, and on the meaningfulness of symptoms, are correct, why would his science not attract public acclaim? Why would he be especially liable to attacks, denunciations, and abuse?

We can best answer these last three questions by considering the detailed analysis of a real case, that of a young woman whose parents sought Freud out with every apparent intention being that he should cure her of her profound suffering. That Freud failed ultimately in that attempt is one of the least important facts about this case history.

II

ON THE REALITY OF PSYCHIC PAIN: THREE CASE HISTORIES

Fragment of an Analysis of a Case of Hysteria
(SE 7) 1905 "Dora"

Notes Upon a Case of Obsessional Neurosis
(SE 10) 1909 "Rat Man"

From the History of an Infantile Neurosis
(SE 17) 1918 "Wolf Man"

Freud's case histories, which have gained a renown that stretches far beyond the confines of psychiatry, may be divided up into two rough categories: those which are reports of his direct work with a patient and those which are essays upon the character of a person whom he did not treat. Members of the first set are the cases published in his and Breuer's *Studies on Hysteria* (1895, SE 2), "Dora" (1905, SE 7), "Rat Man"(1909, SE 10), "Wolf Man" (1918, SE 17), numerous short accounts, and his classic text, *The Interpretation of Dreams*, which contains major portions of his self-analysis. The second set of case histories, those whose subjects were not his patients, includes "Little Hans" (1909, SE 10), "Judge Schreber" (1911, SE 12), as well as his essays on historical personages, like Goethe, and famous literary characters, like Hamlet and, of course, King Oedipus.

The first set is the more valuable for the beginning student of Freud and more pertinent to our aims: to explicate his major claims and to see him at his strength. There is no end to the many fascinating questions raised in and by texts of the second set. His long-distance analysis of "Little Hans," using the boy's father as an intermediary, has spawned a sizeable literature on its own. His many comments on Hamlet and Shakespeare, scattered throughout his writings, are profound and fascinating in their own right. But in all these instances Freud must rely upon either the observations of another person, or, as in the Schreber case, upon written materials from the patient as well as reports about him. These case reports include no systematic record of the patient's associations, nor of the gestures, parapraxes, and other behavioral hints which make up the routine of a long analysis and which provide both parties additional confirmation. Furthermore, there is always something academic about these analyses. They are, necessarily, bookish and take on such didactic roles that reading them is something of a chore.

This is not true of the direct case histories. On the contrary, the three with which we will be concerned, "Dora," "Rat Man," and "Wolf Man," display Freud at his best. They are written with a masterful economy of description, great evocative power, and much wit. Yet they are not mere novels. Their endings are not predictable, they follow no formula, and they have no idealized heroes who after suffering torment and danger rescue pure and chaste heroines. In fact, in the first, "Dora," we struggle along with Freud and his patient only to see the whole enterprise end in failure. Does this make Freud look bad? That judgment must be reserved until we have pondered her story at length.

Fragment of an Analysis of a Case of Hysteria
(SE 7) 1905 "Dora"

1   This is one of the very earliest, lengthy, psychoanalytic case histories to be published. What is Freud's manifest concern, as expressed in these prefatory remarks? And how would you characterize their emotional tone when Freud says that not publishing his findings on hysteria would be a " disgraceful piece of cowardice" (p. 8)?

2   Why would this kind of case be especially liable to be read as a roman à clef (a novel which is a thinly disguised account of famous or infamous people)? Is there something titillating about them, such that some readers might find them as if designed for their private delectation? Is this a mark against their veracity or against Freud's method?

3   One reason Freud gives for publishing this account of a three-month treatment is that it illustrates the technique and therapeutic value of his method of dream interpretation (see above, *Introductory Lectures* numbers V–XV). Yet even for those who understand that technique, the story will prove to be bewildering. Why? What factors give rise to it? Can it ever be removed?

4   Why did Freud change his technique from that of actively confronting the patient's symptoms to more passively waiting for the patient to begin the conversation (p. 13)? Why does this not lead to a state of complete randomness, in which the patient simply meanders from topic to topic? What principle of mental life must be true if one is to accept this as a valid therapeutic method? Given this method, which requires the patient to free associate to his own behavior and thoughts, is Freud's analogy of the archaeologist

entirely accurate? That is, do they also dig randomly and wait for the pieces to come together?

5 Does Freud believe this single case is overwhelmingly supportive of his theory of neurotogenesis (how neuroses are produced)? Does he believe that a single case history fully exhausts the nature and structure of hysteria, that, following him, there is no more to say?

Part I: The Clinical Picture

Technical Terms

Amnesia; paramnesia; unconscious disingenuousness; displacement; conversion; reversal of affect; somatic compliance; secondary function; overdetermination; reinforcement from the unconscious; obsessive

6 As Freud promises the story becomes complex quickly. (It will pay to keep both a record of the various actors arranged in rough chronological order and a chart of Dora's many symptoms, together with Freud's interpretations of them.) He could have made the reader's job a little easier by summarizing the story, explaining its meaning, and altogether giving us a neater package. But he refuses. Why?

7 What universal features of hysteria make it impossible for the honest reporter to give a complete and uninterrupted account of both the patient's history and the patient's treatment? How does this feature permit Freud to distinguish true neuroses from similar, but purely organic, diseases (see pp. 16–17 n. 2)? How does he distinguish unconscious disingenuousness from its counterpart?

8 What permits Freud to say that having repaired the patient's memory (compare paramnesia with amnesia proper), the practical aim of the treatment is also accomplished (p. 18)? How does the patient supply the missing facts which, when recognized, can be fitted into the narration? Could a patient accomplish this alone, without going to the expense and effort of treatment?

9 Now we read the facts about Freud's patient, a young woman he calls "Dora." Here it will be useful to refer to your chart of the family's particular history. In listing these facts about Dora's family does Freud exclude the possibility that her difficulties, especially her physical symptoms, are the results of an unfortunate genetic inheritance? (Which of the family members seems less ill than the others?)

10 We learn that Dora's father had had syphilis before his marriage (p. 20, no. 1). Does Freud consider that to be a factor which may have contributed to Dora's propensity towards psychological illness? How might Dora's mother have responded to the knowledge that her husband had been syphilitic prior to their marriage and

that he might have passed that illness on to their children? What is the popular image of such sexual diseases? Is there some connection, possibly, between those images and her subsequent "housewife psychosis"?

11 In listing some of Dora's physical ailments (pp. 21–12), can one find any thematic relationship that appears to unite them? Were her other physicians ever in doubt as to the diagnosis? Why would someone suffering so many difficulties laugh at the efforts of her doctors to cure her of them?

12 It is often useful to know how persons become patients, and to understand who is most adamant about their need to secure treatment. What sequence of events precipitated Dora's contact with Freud? How is it she was "handed over" for treatment?

13 Whom does Freud believe when it appears, very early in his work, that Dora's story does not always tally with her father's? Is the latter consistent in his own accounts? Is Freud an advocate for either of them?

14 Freud says that he first attempted to apply his and Breuer's trauma theory to this case and to search out, therefore, the actual traumatic event that gave rise to her suicide threat (assuming that that threat was the mark of a "disturbed person"). Yet he does not agree with her father's assessment. He turns back to an event that occurred four years prior to the suicide episode (p. 28). Why does he say Dora's behavior then was "completely hysterical"?

15 This scene, to which both Dora and Freud return an immense number of times in the course of the treatment, is crucial to the entire story and to our judgment of it. Was Herr K abusing Dora when he acted in this way (see p. 29 n. 2)? Contemporary authorities remark upon the frequency of sexual molestation of young children, particularly girls, by older men. Is this such a case?

16 Freud labors to prove that she was hysterical even then and to illustrate the symbolic relationships between the kiss and her subsequent symptoms, including hallucinations. Freud discusses "reversal of affect" and "displacement." Explicate these terms. Does their persistence over a period of four years support or weaken the diagnosis of hysteria?

17 Overtly Dora was shocked and disgusted by Herr K's advance. Freud is sure that part of that shock lay in her perception of his erect penis which in turn is linked to her "oral orientation" toward heterosexual relations. What facts about her father and Frau K and about her own development support Freud's interpretation?

18 Given Freud's understanding of phobias as he developed it in his *Introductory Lectures*, and given a dynamic theory of interpretation, what unconscious wishes and fantasies must underlie and, as

it were, *fuel* a conscious fear of seeing a man's erection? How does a phobia differ from a reaction formation (see *Introductory Lectures*, pp. 375, 381)?

19　Both Dora and her father are intelligent and much beyond the average in the acuity of their judgment and common sense. What tells us Dora is not simply a silly, frightened school girl bullied by more powerful and more intelligent adults? Yet she is neurotic and so "blinded" to other truths. Is her father without psychological impairment?

20　Dora's complaints about her father, Frau K, and Herr K seem legitimate and well taken. Yet Freud makes it a point of his technique to challenge not the veracity of these complaints but their target: on what grounds?

21　One of the great themes that runs throughout this case is that of "silent acquiescence" (p. 37). It would prove instructive to list the characters and their actions who engage in this passive activity. Should Dora's mother be included on this roster? Where was she during all the years Herr K was virtually courting her adolescent daughter?

22　Freud forces Dora to admit that her frequent (hysteric) illnesses coincided with Herr K's absences (p. 39). This is an unconscious sign of the intense love she bore for him. Is it also a positive sign, that is, in general would so intense a response indicate the presence of an overwhelming passion for the beloved? Recall Freud's discussion of parapraxes and other signs of unconscious conflict. He says they are more truthful indicators of one's feelings than sentiments one merely mouths. If Herr K had understood all this ought he have to been optimistic about his future with Dora?

23　How does the concept "somatic compliance" (p. 40) help account for hysteric symptoms? Why, according to this discussion, is there no natural sign language or body language which would convey the same meaning in every instance? Why does it make sense to say hysteric symptoms are overdetermined?

24　Her illness, while overdetermined, has a meaning and so represents a motive. What is that motive, according to Freud? Why does he ask Dora to forgo challenging her father? To protect the latter? Because her father was a powerful man whom he happened to like and so favored over Dora? Is there something else he could have done to "combat her motives" for remaining ill?

25　Why does Freud insist upon treating Dora's rejection of Herr K's advances as a riddle? Why ought Herr K to have trusted the "innumerable small signs" of Dora's affection—at least under more usual circumstances?

26　Follow out Freud's deduction of the meaning of Dora's cough (or at least one of the many meanings expressed by her cough) on pp. 46–47. Dora is not shocked by his questions about oral sexuality, and she answers them easily. Yet Freud says there must come a point in either her recollections or in her associations where she cannot answer. Why? (It might be useful to sketch out Freud's interpretation and diagram the two lines of thought he ascribes to her, both the conscious and unconscious streams.)

27 Note that Freud feels compelled to defend himself from readers who would find his discussions of sexual matters with so young a woman improper and even immoral. What is his defense? (Why does he quote French slogans, why not refer to his favorite poets here?)

28 An ancient bit of wisdom says one should resist condemning the actions or life of another person because "there but for the grace of God go I." A famous psychoanalyst who worked with severely disturbed people said of them "There I go." With whom would Freud agree?

29 When Freud and other dynamic psychologists describe the work of interpreting the meaning of symptoms (or dreams or parapraxes) they frequently use metaphors drawn from linguistics, especially translation. While these two activities are similar, since each is concerned with finding the meaning of a phenomenon which is initially puzzling, why is the metaphor misleading and finally false? (Consider carefully pp. 52–54.) Does the meaning of a Chinese text, for example, suffer the same kinds of changes, reversal, and disconnections that characterize the meaning of Dora's symptoms?

30 Consider the very condensed metaphor about the "reinforcement" of conscious thoughts by excessively intense unconscious thoughts (pp. 54–55). Why is Freud so taken with the galvonometer model as a representation of the relationship between the two trains of thought? Is this a linguistic model, akin to a notion of translation? Given this model and assuming it is valid, does it permit Freud to predict his patient's behavior if there is a likelihood of an unconscious wish arising under certain circumstances? Why would interpretation of the underlying unconscious thought, which means discovering the infantile wish associated with it, help decrease the compulsivity and intensity of the conscious thoughts?

31 What feature of unconscious thoughts in general permits a wish to be represented by an entirely opposite and contrary conscious feeling? Is this a common feature of linguistic signs?

32 On what grounds does Freud conclude that Dora's feelings about her father went beyond the usual bounds of daughterly affection? Is Dora's mother responsible, in part, for the unusual strength of

those feelings? And is her father guilty as well?

33 What can Freud mean when he says that "No other kind of 'Yes' can be extracted from the unconscious; there is no such thing at all as an unconscious 'No'" (p. 57)? If interpreting the unconscious meaning of symptoms and dreams and parapraxes were simply a matter of translating from one language to another, would the "archaic" language of the unconscious be able to represent "No"? This question is worth pursuing for our answer to it will determine how we judge all Freud's later propositions about the uniqueness of psychoanalytic interpretation. What are the consequences for Freud's libido theory if we conclude that unconscious processes are essentially the products of one kind of language operating in a context where it is not yet translated into a language recognized by consciousness? If psychoanalytic interpretation is essentially a linguistic process, what kind of training and education would best prepare one to become a psychoanalyst?

34 But patients have no trouble emitting loud "No's" when confronted by interpretations like the one Freud put to Dora on p. 58. Why ought we to note that her "No" was "most emphatic"? How can a "No" signify "Yes"? Can one find other behaviors or gestures which accomplish a similar feat, that is, represent their opposite? Again, is this a feature of ordinary human languages?

35 By this time an honest reader of Freud's case history and faithful user of these questions will confess that the whole account is immensely frustrating and most obscure. It seems neither very good science, since we can say so little that is absolutely certain about the exact meaning of the various symptoms, nor very good literature since the story is so confused. How does Freud show that the latter, especially, is a sign of his veracity?

36 Freud mentions three women with whom Dora was intimate, perhaps to the point of displaying overtly sexualized feelings. Are there any other females whom we should place among this threesome? Freud says Frau K's betrayal of their secret discussions of sexual matters to Herr K and thereby to her father hurt Dora more than anything else. Is this persuasive? What signs does Freud rely upon to validate this claim?

Part II: The First Dream

Technical Terms

Switch-words; screen memory; primal scene; change of meaning

37 As we have noted before, Freud is not willing to spare his readers the work of carrying out the process of interpretation and suffering

as he did the confusions and frustrations attendant to it. For example, a vital piece of information as well as a helpful bit of theory emerge at the end of this chapter, pp. 92–93. Consequently it will help to read this entire chapter through at least once before attempting to respond to these questions.

38   Note that Freud disallows Dora's objections to her first associations to the dream. Why? What principle of mental functioning allows him to boom out "Start away" (p. 65)?

39   Freud aims to interpret each element of the dream (although later in this chapter he confesses that he overlooked one element). Why is he so keen on establishing when the dream occurred and the number of times it was repeated? Is his guess of four confirmed—directly or indirectly? Note how Freud uses single quote marks around his reports of his and Dora's speeches. What reasons might he have to compose this history in this way?

40   When a murder has occurred there must be a murderer, a means, and a motive. Freud assumes a similar determinism governs the production of a dream: its occurrence and its contents are not random events. How does his insistence upon knowing the number of times the dream was presented lead to his interpretation of one of the intentions which are elements of the latent dream thoughts? The key would seem to be the key.

41   Having established this important bit of reconstruction Freud pauses to recapitulate some major tenets of his theory of interpretation as put forth in *The Interpretation of Dreams*. (Most of which he summarized in the lectures on dreams in the lectures we have read already.) Why does he insert it here, when he is not concerned with the infantile wishes that appear to be part of the dream's larger meaning?

42   When he discusses the jewel case symbol Freud invokes the authority of a "favourite expression" that links it with the female genitals (p. 69). Is this a plausible connection in our culture in our time? Must such symbols be universally interpreted in one way in order for this kind of claim to have merit? How are jewel cases and "reticules," a kind of drawstring bag, related to one another?

43   How does the number of reversals in the dream, where a wish or an idea is converted into its opposite, demonstrate the strength of Dora's feelings? Freud says Dora invoked her oedipal feelings for her father in order to ward off her feelings for Herr K. Would this make sense if one assumes her father is a more taboo object than Herr K?

44   Freud is not finished, for, according to his previous work with dreams, behind this first layer of current (repressed) wishes must lie an even older layer of wishes stemming from childhood. So he uses

the "hint" provided in Dora's concern about an accident occurring in the middle of the night (p. 71). On what authority does he connect the symbol of fire with the problem of bed-wetting? How is the latter connected to her problem with Herr K?

45   Dora reported an addendum to her dream. Why does Freud conclude that it must represent the most repressed dream thoughts? If so, why would her "transference" feelings toward him be the ones she was most afraid of revealing? Why is it that the final interpretation (p. 74) can be stated in a few clear words, while the dream, including its addendum, is obscure, confusing, and disjointed?

46   "No mortal can keep a secret" (p. 77). Does Dora's playing with the string purse prove or merely support Freud's general theory of parapraxes? Why does Venus stand on a shell? (Freud is referring to the famous painting by Botticelli.)

47   In his account of the relationship between masturbation and hysterical symptoms, Freud recalls his analogy of river channels (p. 79). Why would these analogies seem especially appropriate to him, given his general theory of libido? How is masturbation treated in contemporary accounts of childhood and adolescence?

48   The "primal scene" (pp. 79–80) is Freud's name for the child's perception and subsequent representation in memory of adult, usually parental, intercourse. How is it that hysterical actions, like Dora's "dyspnoea" (labored breathing) are remnants of the primal scene? (See the footnote on p. 81.) How might we explain the presence of hand-washing ceremonies. Why would females exhibit hand-washing ceremonies in conjunction with the repression of masturbatory urges? Compare the concept of primal scene with that of screen memory (p. 82 n. 1). Is either a strict photographic representation of a real event? If not, along what lines would one expect such "memories" to be structured?

49   On pp. 83–88 Freud summarizes the factors he feels are responsible for most of Dora's hysteric symptoms (note that he does not doubt she had a most unhappy life). Why is it true to say that Dora fell ill because she was particularly moral, particularly unfortunate, and particularly intelligent? What other route was available to her?

50   Freud then takes up the task of "synthesizing" the dream on pp. 88–93. One excellent way to follow his reasoning is to write out both the manifest and latent dreams and then diagram the ways in which the switch words, like "drops" and "jewel case," connect the first to the second. Does Freud believe that his reconstruction is the only plausible one?

51   A more vexing question reappears in his concluding remarks about the dream's change of meaning (p. 93). (Compare this with

the change of meaning he ascribed to her symptoms, above.) If the manifest dream remains consistent, but its "meanings" change according to Dora's circumstances and feelings, is the dream an ordinary communication?

Part III: The Second Dream

52   So whom did Dora love most? Up until this discussion of her second dream, Freud has only pointed out the variety of people, both male and female, whom Dora loved (or hated). Why must we answer this question? Why can we not give a general answer to it? What additional determinants must we note?

53   Is our view of Herr K and his intentions altered in this chapter? Note that a superficial reading of "Dora" might lead one to suppose that Herr K had simply abused her and treated her only as a sexual conquest. Does Dora (and does Freud) agree?

54   As he had mentioned in the introduction to this case history, Freud's account of the treatment and of how he arrived at his interpretations is not a perfectly coherent set of deductive steps (e.g., p. 93). Why not? Why does he make his reader follow along these winding paths, going from this association to that, rather than simply lay out the dream's "real meaning"? (Again, if a dream were nothing more than a disguised message, would it require so many false starts and stops?)

55   Why does he say the theme of wandering around a strange town was "overdetermined" (p. 96)? What permits Freud to say that Dora's associations to this element really belong to the dream thoughts? (Compare the notion of "nodal point" with that of "switch word," above).

56   As he analyzes the dream point by point Freud first designates a dream element and then Dora's associations (and his reconstructions). Then he links this set of ideas to the next dream element, e.g., on p. 97 he goes from "she asked about a hundred times" to the "contents of the letter." Are these connections simply random or are they brilliant guesses on his part? In other words, how does Freud justify this procedure? (Is it based upon the theory of dream interpretation or upon his knowledge of real life? Is it based on semantic knowledge or encyclopedic knowledge?)

57   Freud usually says that an oddity such as the question mark in front of the word "like" denotes an especially important element in dreams (p. 98). Why would it hold that the more distorted or contorted a dream element the more likely it signifies an important thought? (See his footnote on p. 100 about "endopsychic" resistance.)

58 Freud uses Dora's associations to press her to report again what occurred at the lake. How do her thoughts lead him to make the brilliant reconstruction that Dora must have read a great deal about sexuality in textbooks and consequently knew the technical terms for both male and female genitals?

59 Freud argues that Dora's additional symptom, similar to those associated with appendicitis, was an hysterical elaboration of an actual somatic illness. The final proof being that it appeared nine months after the scene at the lake (p. 103). How would you characterize Freud's attitude toward Dora in these pages? Why does he say "I scarcely dared hope" (p. 103) that Dora would corroborate his solution?

60 The case builds to a finale on pp. 105–108. Dora announces her rejection of the analytic relationship, Freud solves his major puzzle, and gives his final explanation of Dora's hostile rejection of the man she truly loved: "Wounded pride added to jealousy and to the conscious motives of common sense—it was too much" (p. 106). How does Freud present these facts, that is, what stylistic devices does he employ?

61 How does Freud end his narration of the case (p. 109)? Why is there a dash between "She seemed to be moved . . . and—came no more"? What are the "half-tamed demons" (p. 109) with which the analyst must struggle? In what kind of literature would one expect to find demons and such struggling with the hero?

62 Is revenge a dominant motif in Dora's life? How could her breaking off the treatment have harmed Freud? Is revenge a primary motive or a response to a former injustice? Was the treatment a success or a failure? And for whom?

Postscript

Technical Terms

Transference; acting out; sublimation

63 The single most provocative question one can ask of this case history is why did Freud assent to its publication? Not only was the treatment a failure, but he himself is not portrayed in the most winsome way imaginable. So why did he publish it?

64 Would new discoveries about the somatic (physical) sources of mental illness, including the neuroses, dismay Freud? To what does "excitant action" (p. 113) refer? (Note that we do not read Freud's *Three Essays on the Theory of Sexuality* [1905, SE 7] in which he sets out his major observations and theory of infantile sexuality.)

65 "Transference" (pp. 116–117) is a technical term created by Freud
    to designate a certain feature of the analytic relationship. Is trans-
    ference itself a rare ocurrence, appearing only in the intensity of
    psychoanalysis? Why is it more difficult to detect and analyze trans-
    ference elements than it is other elements of the neurosis?

66 Sometimes these revived feelings become conscious and "subli-
    mated" (p. 116). What does this mean and why does Freud call
    these sorts of feelings "revised editions"? How are transference
    feelings and "acting out" (p. 119) connected so that one might say
    that acting out precludes insight?

67 Freud implies it was his technical errors that precipitated Dora's
    sudden withdrawal from treatment. Do you agree? How would
    you characterize his feelings toward Dora, particularly after she
    had announced her decision? Note his attitude toward her when
    she returned fifteen months later: "I could not help smiling; for I
    was able to show her that exactly a fortnight [fourteen days] ear-
    lier she had read a piece of news that concerned me in the news-
    paper" (pp. 121–122). Why can he not stop himself from smiling?
    (On the relationship between Dora and Freud see Erikson [1962]
    and Deutsch [1957].)

Notes Upon a Case of Obsessional Neurosis
(SE 10) 1909 "Rat Man"

As he said in his introduction to "Dora," Freud recognizes that he
has not arranged these case histories in the most readable manner. These
are not textbook accounts, designed to initiate the student into a well
documented mode of study the methods and findings of which are compatible with common sense and received opinion. On the contrary, the
"crumbs of knowledge" (p. 157) each contains were won at the cost of
arduous labor and immense patience. We, his readers, will have to exert
a modicum of effort along the same line that connects the oddities and
incoherencies of the Rat Man's manifest behavior with the deeper strata
of his latent motives.

Given that it took Freud, a man of wide learning and striking talent,
a month to organize the case history, it seems not unreasonable that we
may have to spend a few hours of work in comprehending it.

Introduction & The Beginning of the Treatment

Technical Terms

Flight into illness; mesalliance; nuclear complex; obsessive ideas;
delirium; compulsive behavior; prohibitions; reconstruction; scopophilia;
protective measures

1 Dora's analysis took about fourteen weeks; the one described here took around a year. But does Freud believe the record he presents is complete and that it describes fully the nature of obsessional neurosis? Would a purely deductive science admit of so many gaps and, sometimes, inconsistencies within its propositions?

2 Having read "Dora" we will want to compare her story and Freud's analysis of it to the young man who, thanks to his outstanding obsessional fear about rats, is known universally as the "Rat Man." (If that name offends one he is also referred to as Dr. Lorenz in the addendum, p. 254). Compare the ways in which both came to visit Freud for their first consultation. Why is Dr. L's more propitious than Dora's? How does Freud feel about Dr. L?

3 Freud says he made the patient "pledge" to say everything that came into his head (this is also termed the basic rule). What great principle of mental functioning, elucidated in the *Introductory Lectures*, underlies this pledge? Are there any other disciplines or treatments or relationships in which one party is required to pledge absolute candor? Are these therapeutic relationships?

4 Outline Dr. L's description of his life in the first hour (a full hour—why could Dora not have produced so coherent and complete an account in her first hour with Freud?). Why does Freud say that his patient was already an obsessional neurotic at age six? Why is the presence of sexual urges and aggressive wishes not sufficient to produce an infantile neurosis? A significant element in the definition of obsessional neurosis is the compulsive and repetitive quality of the patient's actions. Given what we know of Dr. L's boyhood (pp. 162–163), how can we account for these irrational repetitions?

5 Although there is no doubt that the patient was obsessional at age six, the link between his wishes and his fears, even at that age, is not clear. What will "reconstruction" bring about?

6 Freud's account of the "Great Obsessive Fear" is a marvelous piece of dramatic reportage (note he gives us both dialogue and scene). Why is Dr. L's "composite expression" (p. 166) a key to understanding the whole story? What can "horror at pleasure of his own" (p. 167) mean? Given this observation of manifest behaviors, what must we conclude about the latent thoughts of which they are expressions?

7 The obsessional idea is revealed in much of its absurdity by the patient's admission of the second, concurrent fantasy about his father suffering the same rat punishment. Then comes the matter of the money the "cruel" captain had told him to pay Lieutenant A. To which elements in "Dora" ought we to compare this memory/fantasy of the money owed to Lt. A? (As in that history,

so here too it will pay to keep a chart or list of the ideas and memories that the patient links to this nodal point.)

8   Dr. L addresses Freud as "Captain" during his recitation of these events. Why? Are there similar events in daily life when normal persons may find themselves addressing someone incorrectly? What feelings typify this kind of parapraxis? (Note that during such moments the patient speaks well but as if in a dream [p. 170]).

9   Did Dr. L wish to become a patient? How did he arrive at Freud's doorstep? Why would the chance event of reading one of Freud's books serve him in his efforts at finding help? Was it a chance event—given what we know about parapraxes and other apparently accidental behaviors?

10 Freud terms these first sessions an initiation into the treatment. Is it fair to say that they are also initiations into the theory of psychoanalysis? Is Freud's metaphor about Pompei and the unconscious persuasive? Is it entirely accurate? If yes, would that mean that there would be no hints or traces of the "buried" thoughts and wishes observable in the patient's everyday conscious behavior?

11 At the end of their fourth session Freud summons up his thoughts and gives a prognosis (p. 178). Given what he has said already about the validity of affective responses which, although tied to inconsequential or even ridiculous thoughts, point to authentic wishes, how should we assess the fact that Dr. L responds with "visible pleasure" to Freud's good opinion of him?

12 How is the quantity of affection an important element in the generation of Dr. L's obsessional ideas about his father's death? Given Freud's reasoning would we expect to find obsessional ideas surrounding persons of no consequence to oneself? (And given what we know of transference, what kind of feelings might we expect the patient to exhibit toward Freud when the treatment reaches the depths of the patient's unconscious?)

13 Why does the age, as it were, and intensity of his infantile feelings make them so recalcitrant? Note that most neurotic symptoms are irrational behaviors that appear trivial both to the neurotic and to his acquaintances. (Recall Freud's favorite metaphor of the unconscious as a burial ground of ancient relics.)

14 After castigating himself and his motives, Dr. L admits to his deep feelings of cowardice, to which Freud responds. And then, in the footnote, Freud would appear to disown his arguments as ineffective (p. 185). But were they? How might the patient have experienced these admonitions?

15 In part E, "Some Obsessional Ideas and Their Explanation," Freud describes six well-defined symptoms, then explains their common

origin. Summarize the six symptoms, show their interior logic, and, if possible, arrange them along a line of severity. Freud often speaks of "translating" these ideas into their actual or original motives (e.g., p. 186). Is "translation" a correct term for the work he and his patient do in this analysis?

16   Obsessional neurotics manifest a deep ambivalence toward significant persons, as do hysterics. Why do the former "construct" their symptomatic expressions differently than the latter? Why would one repress hostile feelings toward someone more readily than one would repress affectionate ones? Freud notes that people may laugh during a funeral or upon hearing of the death of a loved one. Are there similar instances of inappropriate mirth in ordinary life? How might we explain them?

17   In part F, "The Precipitating Cause of the Illness," Freud compares the logic and genesis of obsessive symptoms with those of hysteria. Why is the archaeology metaphor, about Pompeii, for example, even less appropriate to a correct understanding of obsession than it is to hysteria? How does Freud distinguish the two kinds of repression as well as two kinds of knowledge that typify obsessives (see the note on p. 196)?

18   In the story of his other client who ironed his money while abusing the trust of his friends Freud concludes that the man had displaced his self-reproach because an accurate self-understanding would inhibit his one avenue of sexual pleasure. Why is it plausible to suppose that the latter was based upon "infantile determinants" (p. 198)?

19   Freud says Dr. L became ill, as an adult, precisely when he had to resolve a conflict that paralleled an event in his father's young manhood (pp. 198–199). How did Freud use the transference elements to convince his patient of the correctness of this interpretation? (Compare Freud's use of the transference here and on p. 209, with his failure with Dora on similar issues.)

20   Returning to the theme of infantile and adolescent masturbation, Freud seems convinced there must be some meaning to Dr. L's bizarre actions upon the midnight hour (p. 204). Why is he convinced that these must have infantile precursors? Are we "astonished" too by the patient's response?

21   Why is the work of analysis a "school of suffering"? Could Freud have made it any easier or more pleasant for his patient? How did he remain calm and neutral when he and his family were subjected to so many verbal abuses? Would a clever patient, such as Dr. L, not have found at least a few weak spots in Freud's character or in his family and so directed his insults toward a real, and therefore vulnerable, point?

22   How are the German words "Spielratte," "Ratten," "Raten," and
      "hieraten," connected together in the patient's mind? What kind
      of connections are these? That is, could one have predicted their
      appearance? Would an excellent knowledge of German have
      allowed one to predict their occurrence in such a story? If not,
      what additional information would one require? Why does Freud
      refer to Goethe (p. 216) and to Ibsen and fairy tales in connection
      with the theme of rats?

23   Note that the interpretation of the obsessional idea is exactly like
      that of the interpretation of the manifest dream content: Freud
      aims to account both for the latent content and for the distortions
      of that content by the censorship. What crime had Dr. L commit-
      ted (in his thoughts) such that the torturous trip from P to Z, etc.,
      was the fitting punishment?

24   Is Freud claiming that any young man, faced with a similar situa-
      tion (the error about the money he owed), would have concocted
      so elaborate an obsessional drama? What appear to be the deter-
      minate factors, summarized in this section, that together produced
      Dr. L's neurotic actions? If one could have known these factors
      before the events with the cruel captain, could one have also
      predicted exactly which ideas and which fantasies would have
      appeared in his deliria?

25   If one could not predict the exact content of a patient's (or experi-
      mental subject's) obsessional ideas, does that mean there is no
      objective way to verify the correctness of Freud's interpretations?
      How did Dr. L respond to them? Is this kind of response an ade-
      quate verification of so elaborate a theory?

Theoretical: General Characteristics
of Obsessional Structures

Technical Terms

Primary and secondary defense; omnipotence of thoughts; reaction formations; undoing; isolation; ambivalence; regression; sexualization of
thoughts

26   While reading Freud or another author concerned with the eluci-
      dation of neurotic behavior one may feel inexplicably tired, or
      distracted, or bored even though one is overtly interested in the
      subject matter. Why might this occur? For example, a young man
      might find it necessary to re-read a passage in this case history
      many times before he was able to understand it. Suggest some
      lines of inquiry about this kind of event—would we be justified in
      considering it an example of an obsessional structure (p. 221)?

27   How does Freud distinguish between the primary defensive strug-
      gle and the secondary defensive efforts that come after it? Why
      would patients "tone down" the distinction between wishes, inten-
      tions, doubts, etc. and call them all "ideas" (p. 223)?

28   During the secondary struggle the patient creates new ideas which
      Freud terms obsessional structures, or, more technically, "deliria"
      (p. 222). Why does he say these are structures, rather than simply
      trains of thought or groups of ideas? Does the secondary struggle
      issue in a "tertiary" struggle in therapy (cf. "the disease plucks up
      courage" on p. 223)?

29   A famous French psychoanalyst once advised that solving cross-
      word puzzles would be good practice for young analysts. Does this
      make sense to you? Compare two or three of the patient's protec-
      tive formulas with a crossword puzzle: Are they identical?

30   Freud says jokes, dreams, and obsessional formula may all exhibit
      an identical structure: the use of ellipsis (pp. 226–228). Compare
      the joke on p. 227 with an obsessional idea (from this case history
      or elsewhere). Why is it that most people can "get" the joke, and
      are pleased by it, while very few people can interpret correctly
      the obsessional idea (and if they do are repelled by the latent
      thought)?

31   From the beginning, Freud and his science have been subjected to
      numerous philosophic critiques, some sophisticated and intelli-
      gent, others ill-informed and vicious. Why would he appear so
      vulnerable to rationalist critics? Is he? Another famous French
      thinker said that he found himself changed, for the better, by his
      careful reading of Freud. Does this make sense? Would philoso-
      phers in general have a special concern about obsessional actions?

32   After describing typical superstitious beliefs Freud explains the
      difference between two types of repression: one that effects a state
      of amnesia, another that severs "causal connections" (p. 231).
      Which is typical of obsessives? Consider two or three examples of
      superstitious behavior (including those typical of groups as well as
      individuals). Are these similar to Dr. L's obsessive structures?
      (Freud addresses this issue at length in "The Uncanny," which we
      consider below.)

33   How does a belief in the "omnipotence of wishes" typify the
      obsessive's mental life? In what other circumstances, or in what
      kind of literature or cultural artifacts do you find a similar
      emphasis upon the power of wishes? It happens that L had a
      number of experiences in which his wishes for the death of a rival
      were granted (e.g., p. 234). Does this mean that such events con-
      vinced him of his special power, that they were partly responsible
      for his becoming neurotic? If not, how should we understand the

frequency with which Freud's obsessive patients report such "uncanny" experiences?

34 Surely many young men experience difficulties similar to those of Dr. L. Why are they all not obsessive and indecisive? In other words, what is the relationship between Dr. L's adult neurosis and his childhood conflicts with his father? Why is Freud convinced that it was the repression of Dr. L's infantile hatred for his father that underlay the later neurosis? Was that hatred sui generis or was it, at least in part, related to the "nuclear complex"?

35 On pp. 240ff. Freud makes a few conjectures about the source of the intense hatred obsessional neurotics manifest as children: Does he rule out a biological or physiological source? He then lists three factors responsible for the insidious way this primal hatred (combined with a primal love) comes to dominate the patient's life. Which of these three appears to be the most important?

36 While Freud uses the term repression here as he did in "Dora," we have seen that it refers to a distinct process in which the infantile wish persists but is altered radically. Why? Given this second kind of repression, what may we conclude about the accuracy of Freud's reconstructions when we learn that L showed the "most violent resistance" (p. 238) when Freud touched upon his hatred for his father?

37 Freud's patient had quoted Nietzsche's famous dictum: "'I did this,' says my Memory, 'I cannot have done this,' says my Pride and remains inexorable. In the end—Memory yields" (p. 184). How does the structure of memory lend itself to the obsessional's aims? (Trace the sequence of perception, psychic pain, memory, doubt, and repression and then repetition that issued in one of Dr. L's symptoms.)

38 Why, according to Freud's discoveries, is it correct to say that obsessive actions are instances of "regression" (p. 244)? Does this mean that all children will manifest beliefs and hence protective measures similar to those Dr. L produced? Around what kinds of themes would one expect to find childish superstitions and protective rituals centered? Examine two or three examples of children's games: Do you find obsessive features in them similar to those Freud found in Dr. L's behavior? Given Freud's general understanding of the source of such actions, what kinds of behavior will an especially superstitious child exhibit if he or she is placed under severe emotional strain?

39 Consider Freud's formula on p. 246: an obsessive thought represents an action regressively. What factors in the Rat Man case history support his contention that every thought (or "idea") has two sides, an economic one and a representational one? How is it

that an obsessive patient like Dr. L may recognize easily an idea that the analyst has laboriously reconstructed, yet remain unimpressed by its relevance to his neurotic conflicts?

40   In his conclusion Freud says his patient has, as it were, disintegrated into three personalities (pp. 248–249). Does he mean to imply that there were three distinct personalities operating within one body? Is this latter idea so foreign to lay persons or, indeed, to children? How might we understand the presence of so many doubles, twins, good witches vs. bad witches, and ghosts in children's stories? (We reconsider this great question, and its relevance to religious myth, below in our discussion of "The Uncanny").

Original Record of the Case
(SE 10, pp. 253–318)

Although Freud never intended that his notes be published, we are extremely fortunate to have them. They show Freud's mind at work, one of the wonders of this century, and they give us a much fuller portrait of the patient's day-to-day life. They also permit us to ask a number of additional questions, the answers to which will help explain the hints Freud makes about the connection between his patient's great fear about the rats and the general topic of anal sexuality.

41   It will have struck the reader new to Freud that his patients seem to be extraordinarily concerned about the smells, products, and state of their genitals and the status of others' as well. We recall the fascination and dread about genital secretions that marked Dora's thoughts about herself, e.g., the switch-word "drops." So too, Dr. L's associations are tied to genitals, feces, urine, semen, blood, odors, and other kinds of discharge. Is this peculiar to neurotics or to nineteenth-century Vienna? How are these body products treated in our culture? (Are they in some way still magical substances?)

42   In a similar way, Dr. L's transference fantasies about Freud and members of Freud's family are distinctly scatological. In what extra-analytic circumstances does one find scatological comments to abound? Who in our culture and what professions are especially concerned with odors and fragances?

43   Compare Dr. L's equation of rats and money and his fascination with anal imagery with the major themes of the play and film "Guys and Dolls." In the latter the big gambling scene takes place in a giant underground sewer. Why does this make psychological sense (was the movie a crap out or did it bring in buckets of money)?

44   Among the fascinating accounts of the transference interaction

Freud mentions that he had once given his patient some food (pp. 311, 314–315). This elicits a great many fantasies from the patient. Why? On p. 303 Freud simply tells us he was hungry and was fed (note that their two families were distantly known to one another).

45   Assuming the reader of these questions has made it through these two case histories it cannot fail to impress him or her that they are about actions and thoughts that verge on the disgusting, and are almost always in the worst of taste. Must this be so? Compare these fantasies and wishes with the overt actions in children's TV shows in this culture. Is it easier to watch a cops and robbers show than it is to read "Dora" or "Rat Man"? Why might this be so?

From the History of an Infantile Neurosis
(SE 17) 1918 "Wolf Man"

Although this case history, popularly known as the "Wolf Man" in honor of the patient's dream about wolves, is Freud's longest and most detailed, it lacks the breathless quality of urgent discovery that characterizes both "Dora" and "Rat Man." One reason for this is Freud's didactic efforts to defend his science against his critics Jung and Adler, both of whom had been his collaborators. These efforts, especially chapter five, are not mere polemics. On the contrary, Adler's rationalist critique, especially, is important because it exemplifies contemporary philosophic opinions about psychoanalysis and hence Freud's response is as pertinent now as it was then.

Yet the case is a vivid and fascinating account of the life of a real human being whose inner turmoil is captured in Freud's account and made intelligible to us. It is an ideal bridge text since it connects Freud's strictly clinical theories with larger questions about the social and cultural factors that influence each of us. More so, it contains an extended analysis of the boy's religion (chapter six) and so takes us to our final consideration of Freud's essays on religion proper.

Introduction (I)
and General Survey of the Case (II)

Technical Terms

Primal scene; deferred reaction; screen memory; narcissism; passive/active aims; bisexuality; sublimation

1   Although Freud says he cannot hope to give a complete and full account of this long case, which lasted four years, any more than he could of that of Dora, which lasted fourteen weeks, the story is remarkably coherent. (On first reading it may help to jot down

the chronology he sets out on p. 121 in chapter nine.) The title of the case history suggests we are to follow the investigation of a child's mind via psychoanalysis. Yet the patient is a young man! How does Freud defend both his title and the claims he intends to make about his patient as a boy?

2   Freud summarizes the boy's history: he passed from anxiety-hysteria (tied to an animal phobia), to obsessional neurosis (tied to strict religious observances), to a final collapse when he was seventeen (p. 8). Assuming this is an accurate sketch, compare the nature of psychiatric "diseases" with that of others. Can chicken pox turn into pneumonia and that into some other distinct disease?

3   Freud has other reasons for publishing this case history: to explicate his claim about the libidinal component and the absence of "any aspirations towards remote cultural aims" (p. 9). What must his assumptions be about the development of adult sexuality and adult personality in general such that he can confidently "postdict" the nature of his patient's infantile sexuality and infantile personality? (Recall the passages in the *Introductory Lectures* regarding the question of psychic determinism.)

4   What is the "attachment to myself" that Freud says was of major importance in his effort to overcome his patient's resistance? Why would the hypnotic-like lucidity Freud's tactic engendered be of special significance in this case of retrospective analysis? (Compare it to Dora's usual mode of communication.)

5   It sometimes happens that an ardent neurotic will suddenly change, drop all symptoms, and achieve something like normal psychological functioning. For example, some neurotics became true heroes in the midst of concentration camps. Does this mean that therefore they were not really ill to begin with and that all they really needed was the correct exhortation or challenge? Given his analogy of the army fighting across a piece of land, how would Freud account for such dramatic moments of healing? (Would this be true of religious cures, as well?)

General Survey of the Patient's Environment and the History of the Case

III: The Seduction and Its Immediate Consequences

6   In summarizing the story Freud says his patient threw all the incidents around his "naughty period" into a jumbled mess (p. 15). Why would he do so at the beginning of his analysis? (Note that as in "Rat Man" the case history includes a dominant theme of religious concerns that are somehow tied up with anal fantasies.)

7   The patient reports two "screen memories" (p. 19). Are these

accurate memories of an actual event? If not, why does the patient experience them as if they were? And why would they be repeated so many times and have such strong feelings attached to them? Why are dreams repeated? What caused the dreams reported on this page?

8   Why would the boy's initiation into sexual play by his older sister offend his masculine self-esteem? When would such damage most likely occur? Why is the issue of passivity and activity of such importance here? If his sister had been the guilty party, why would the little boy rage at the English governess and not his sister? Why did he not report the "outrage" to either the governess or his Nanya? (Compare his reaction to his sister's death with his homage to the great poet.)

9   As Freud mentions in the beginning section of the case history, ardent skeptics of psychoanalytic claims will not be persuaded by this short account. Which items of the seduction drama will appear most unlikely to the naive or skeptical reader? How does the boy acquire more and more confirmation of the reality of castration? How does it happen that so many children's stories lend themselves to these kinds of interpretations?

10   The theme of passivity reappears in this section when Freud explains why the boy (1) concocted masochistic fantasies about being struck on the penis, (2) had sexual longings for his father (in which he vaguely pictured himself as receiving something from his father), and (3) fell away from the genital level of psychosexual functioning. How does the threat and "reality" of castration figure into each of these passive responses? Are all children capable of such passive traits?

11   How does the boy change the meaning of his screaming fits when his father returns? Is corporal punishment tinged with or related to sexual or erotic feelings? What facts of adult sexual life support (or refute) this association of violence and sexuality? (Looking forward, how does the infant's perception of the primal scene prefigure this later aggressive desire to be beaten by his father?)

IV: The Dream and the Primal Scene

12   The first three pages of this chapter are excerpts from Freud's essay on dreams and fairytales (1913d). Note that immediately after relating the dream the patient says it took a long time for him to realize it was only a dream, and not a real perception (p. 29). Why will Freud hold that this is an important clue as to the reality of the primal scene? (The associations that follow are beautiful examples of dream interpretation.)

13 In addition to this clue, Freud accepts his patient's emphasis upon the stillness of the wolves and how attentively they peered at him (p. 34). Together with these clues he lists the theme of castration, sexual problems, his father and something terrible (p. 34). How does Freud get from this set of factors to the central intepretation on p. 37? What principles from the interpretation of dreams help us explain how the boy transformed the sight of his parents copulating in bed into a vision of the wolves sitting in the trees?

14 The evidence suggests that the boy witnessed his parents copulating one afternoon when he was about a year and a half. Yet his anxiety dream occurred two and a half years later, when he was about four! Is this a problem for Freud's interpretation of the dream? How does he propose to account for such a "deferred reaction" (p. 38)? Later, we learn, the boy had a Latin teacher named Wolf. Does this mean that "fate" was against him? (Compare this piece of fate with the Rat Man's propensity for finding uncanny connections between his thoughts and external occurrences.)

15 As we learned in the lectures on dream interpretation, Freud does not consider a dream to be interpreted fully until each element in the dream is accounted for and until one can re-express the manifest dream in straightforward language: the latent dream thoughts. What thoughts underlie the wolf dream?

16 How did his mother and father "become wolves"? Are there similar themes of animals losing their tails, or some other extremity in fairy tales and folk literature? If so, how did they arise? Ought parents and teacher to excise them from the curriculum? Compare the number and kinds of monsters with which contemporary children are fascinated—are they similar to the wolves and other sadistic animals of the Wolf Man's childhood?

V: A Few Discussions, and

VI: The Obsessional Neurosis

17 Freud recounts the three major problems that confront his reconstruction of the latent dream thoughts which, when transformed by the dream work, issued in the anxiety dream. He then attempts to solve them. Why is the "rationalization" of infantile sexuality (p. 49) so attractive? And why, even if events like the seduction and witnessing of the primal scene were merely adult fantasies ascribed to an early period, would analysis proceed in exactly the same manner?

18 Freud's answer contains the surprising thesis that it is precisely the fact that the analyst must reconstruct them that argues in favor of their authenticity. Why does this "single admission" not decide the

whole dispute? Why does the recurrence of material in dreams support his claim about the reality of the reported experiences? What single principle of mental functioning, again, underlies Freud's confidence in his formulation of the "laws of dream-formation" (p. 51)?

19 Another obvious and important objection to Freud's general thesis is the assertion that since psychoanalysts are so committed to a "depth" theory, and have themselves been initiated, as it were, into the "cult" of analysis, they will ascribe necessarily a fixed set of fantasies to their patients and so find "confirmation" of what they themselves created. How does Freud answer this frequent charge? Do other scientists demand that their critics acquire a firsthand knowledge of the facts before they launch their critical demands? Would this hold for the philosophic critics of analysis as well?

20 Yet another problem emerges for Freud when he addresses the task of answering Adler and Jung, both of whom were experienced analysts and therefore, presumably, had met Freud's initial demands, above. Is Freud denying what they say is true? If not, what is their error? How would one go about verifying or falsifying Freud's claims that Adler and Jung could not tolerate the truly revolutionary aspects of analysis?

21 In the addendum, pp. 57–60, Freud reconsiders the problem of the reality of the primal scene, since there is evidence that the boy may have observed sheep dogs copulating in the manner and with the frequency that his fantasy ascribes to his parents. After considering these arguments Freud gives his characteristic response, "I can tolerate the charge of absurdity," and says the question remains marked by a non liquet (p. 60). Why use this judicial metaphor here?

22 In chapter six we read how the boy employed his religious instruction in support of his major anxieties. As Freud admits, the boy's original criticisms and questions about the Bible story, the Christian story, were especially keen—so much so that Freud attempted to convince his patient that he had incorrectly ascribed adult skepticism and critical powers to his boyhood. How does Freud account for this precociousness?

23 How does the first sublimation, through religious identifications, differ from the second? Why does the first give rise to obsessional symptoms, e.g., the bedtime rituals? Are these "overdetermined"? Is the persistence of ritualization in religion a sign of successful or unsuccessful sublimation? (Freud, of course, addresses these questions in his texts on religion which we discuss below.)

24 What are the two ambivalent feelings that "were to rule the whole of his later life" (p. 66)? How did the boy come to identify

the Holy Ghost (*hagios pneuma*) with his father and him in turn with an evil spirit who threatened bodily harm? Would this kind of identification occur in all young boys undergoing Christian instruction? Why not? To understand more fully the link between the Christian story and his symptoms diagram how the young boy recasts the religious data along the lines of his earliest concerns.

25 Why was the new sublimation, effected under his German tutor, a better one? Was it constructed for the same purposes as the first? Given this rudimentary explication of the meaning of the term, can we say that analysis itself fosters sublimations or that it replaces them with something else? How does the patient's response to therapy differ from his response to the religious and then the military sublimations of his homosexual interests?

VII: Anal Eroticism and the Castration Complex, and

VIII: Fresh Material from the Primal Period-Solution

26 The translator rightly refers us to Freud's essay on "Character and Anal Eroticism," for there he explains some of the extraordinary facts he simply mentions in this case history. Yet having read "Rat Man," and having reflected upon the pervasiveness of anality in our culture, we can plunge ahead. (On the connection between money and anality see chapter three in Fisher and Greenberg, 1977.)

27 Consider the evidence Freud adduces linking his patient's fascination with money to his dread of his father (he mentions at least seven distinct examples). Why does his lack of knowledge about his actual expenditures and his bank balance suggest that he has attached unconscious wishes to all his monetary dealings?

28 How did his bowels "join in the conversation" (p. 76) with the work of the analysis? Since feces are connected in our adult culture as well as in the patient's adult life with money, does it follow that feces and the bowels in general always had this significance? How, according to this argument, did the patient come to use his bowels as a means of identifying himself with his mother?

29 Freud does not overlook the contradiction engendered by his two distinct interpretations of the meaning of the bowel symptoms. Why are unconscious processes capable of such contradictions, while conscious ones are not? What psychical mechanism allows us to explain how the boy retained these two incompatible theories—the cloacal one and the vaginal one? If the former is widely held, what kind of games or dreams or fantasies might we expect to see associated with it?

30 Given Freud's general theory of mental functioning, why does he

conclude that his patient's sudden bowel problems, during their joint investigations of his anal birth theories, are confirmations of their reconstruction of the primal scene? (Compare the sudden appearance of "transitory symptoms" with Freud's conjecture that the boy's father may have scolded him—perhaps threatening violent punishment—when he soiled himself.)

31   How is his "sordid avarice" (p. 83) and the intensity with which he accused his mother and sister of greed a measure of his anxiety? More specifically, what permits Freud to conclude (p. 84) that the young boy's fear of castration was allayed by and somehow transformed into the eroticization of the fecal mass?

32   From this immensely odd condensation of feces, penis, and baby into one unconscious representation, the patient concocted a sequence of representations of castration (pp. 85–88). Why is his obsessional relationship to his tailors an especially good clue as to the reality of this unconscious fear?

33   Chapter eight contains an account of the final interpretations which effected a cure of his patient. Furthermore, Freud extends his attempts to distinguish his method from those of Jung, Adler and rationalist philosophers who attempt to use the standards and modes of conscious psychology to account for neurotic behavior. It may help to diagram the differences between Freud's initial interpretation of the butterfly's stripes (p. 89) with the much more complex and idiosyncratic one that the patient eventually produces (pp. 90–91).

34   Could anyone have predicted a child would come to associate the hour of five in the evening with the Roman V, and that with a butterfly wing moving, and those in turn with a woman in sexual passion? Is the prediction of the organism's future behavior a crucial task of any authentic science? If analysts cannot predict consistently their patients' behavior, what constrains them from offering an infinite number of ad hoc "post dictions"? Could the patient himself perhaps have done this under Freud's insistence and, like a poet, simply fabricated a plausible connection between truly random elements? (Consider how the patient fell into violent love and consider how the treatment ended.)

35   Freud has some sheep dog characteristics himself. Having reported the patient's beautiful dream of the "Espe" (p. 94), he returns to the nagging question of the authenticity of the primal scene (p. 95). How could one decide the question of the boy's feelings when he was two-and-a-half and urinating in front of Grusha? If this is not decidable, what kind of additional information or support would one require in order to answer these kinds of questions? (Freud's reflections on the phylogenetic heritage will emerge with more

force in *Totem and Taboo*, which we discuss below.)

36 Freud then returns to one of his patient's most idiosyncratic pronouncements: that he experienced the world as if hidden from it by a veil (p. 75 in the SE text). Given the complexity of this element it will pay one to chart out the associations the patient brings to bear upon it. At the same time it is worth noting what it does not include: Freud's hypothesis linking the torn veil with the tearing of the hymen of a virgin is not pertinent (p. 101, n.). Why not?

37 How does Freud arrive at his conclusion, which is also a final formulation of the meaning of the adult's neurosis, that the fantasy underlying the Wolf Man's symptoms was one of copulation with a powerful male? How does the lifting of the veil correlate with this extraordinary fantasy? (Is it extraordinary?)

38 The libido theory, in all its manifestations, has been criticized from the beginning as either much too abstract, since it refers to energies one can never measure objectively, or much too concrete, since it entails claims about the "organ" source of psychological energy. Yet Freud clung to it, just as he clings to his more difficult and improbable views on the primal scene. Why? If there were no such thing as anal eroticism, what status could we give to Freud's interpretations and reconstructions in this case?

IX: Recapitulations and Problems

39 In summarizing his presentation Freud delimits carefully what he feels his science can account for and what remains beyond its ken: Why can one case not exhaust all possible elements of the psyche? Compare the method of analysis with that of microscopic investigation: Why can the former not pretend to the clarity and certainty of the latter? Why, for example, is the distinction between conscious and unconscious processes not a stable indicator of the accuracy of reconstructions? What other sciences have these kinds of difficulties?

40 "Whenever he shrank back onto the transference from the difficulties of the treatment, he used to threaten me with eating me up and later with all kinds of other ill-treatment" (pp. 106–107). How does this kind of example support Freud's roundabout description of the primacy of the oral phase? What other kinds of evidence would you require before granting him this claim? (Note the editor's reference to Freud's *Three Essays* [1905, SE 7].)

41 How can we distinguish a conflict between sexual urges and the ego as a whole (what Freud terms here the moral ego) and a conflict between active and passive sexual impulses? Why are the latter not identical with masculine and feminine sexual currents

(that is, with bisexuality)? Finally, how do we know that the "sadistic-anal" phase persisted and triumphed even as the boy entered puberty?

42 Freud's major goal is to document the ways in which an original anxiety hysteria was transformed into an obsessional neurosis, which in turn underlay the patient's collapse in his late teenage years. We see the pieces fit into place only in the last part of the analysis (and in the last part of Freud's exposition). Why? Why would the final key to the neurotic conundrums appear only at the end of the analysis?

43 Did religion offer the boy any help at all in his difficulties? What "incomparable sublimation" did the Passion story offer the young boy? Freud says three things militated against his ability to adopt a religious solution (pp. 117–118). Which of these is the most significant? Could the patient have become aware of his strong homosexual yearnings without the benefit of analysis? That is, what elements in his theory would Freud have to revise if we were to show him a case similar to this, including its religious dimensions, in which the patient was fully aware of his homosexual longings?

44 Is the "narcissistic" frustration Freud ascribes to his patient's bout with venereal disease a product of the breakthrough of instinctual forces alone, or is it something additional? What other indications do we have that his narcissistic feelings were excessive? Freud says his patient did not achieve a complete sublimation through his religious devotions and practices. Does this mean that another person, one less ill or with better luck, might have done what the Wolf Man could not? Might religious institutions provide avenues for the sublimation of narcissistic feelings, even excessive ones?

We consider these latter questions when we contemplate Freud's analysis and critique of religion. We will see that religion is one of Freud's lifelong concerns. Freud was not a shallow rationalist psychologist nor was he a shallow rationalist critic of religion. The sheer volume of his works on religion documents the intellectual intensity he expended upon its elucidation. However, before we can understand completely the nature and extent of that critique we must first comprehend his general theory of culture. One way to accomplish that task is to read critically his major short essays on the relationship between the individual and civilization. Principal among these is his wonderful essay, "The Uncanny."

III
THE CRITIQUE OF RELIGION
"The Uncanny" (SE 17) 1919

Totem and Taboo (SE 13) 1912–13

Group Psychology and the Analysis of the Ego
(SE 18) 1921

The Future of an Illusion (SE 21) 1927

Moses and Monotheism (SE 23) 1939

As I suggested in the introduction to this study, many traditionalists in religious studies and other non-psychiatric disciplines will find my approach to Freud frustrating. Why take the long road to a critical reading of his texts on religion when his official statement about religion, *The Future of an Illusion*, is readily available? Having tried to teach something about Freud's thought for seven years, I find three things fundamentally wrong with this traditionalist position and therefore with the usual humanistic approach to Freud (particularly that of philosophers and theologians).

First, Freud's genius is not that of an abstract thinker. Rather it is that of the perceptive and revolutionary observer whose discoveries, like that of Columbus, are contrary to received opinion. *The Future of an Illusion* does not constitute his greatest gift to Western thinking (his place in history is assured without it).

Second, one cannot properly understand the sweep and authority of his psychoanalytic claims—as opposed to his philosophic claims—without having spent some time laboring in the vineyards of self-observation, dream interpretation, and, ideally, personal therapeutic experience. All his thoughts on religion are the results of applied psychoanalysis—a fact to which he readily admits. They are hypothetical in the extreme and so depend for their authority upon the clinical theory elucidated in part in the three great case histories we studied above.

Third, psychoanalysis is primarily an observational science whose practitioners remain committed to fulfilling the general requirements of scientific objectivity and rigor. And for that reason all honest analytic theorists admit that some formulations, for example about the absolute source of neurotic symptoms, are conjectures, while others are well established theorems, for example that obsessions and anality are inexorably tied together. While some notable attempts have been made to formalize psychoanalytic theory, no one would claim they have been completely successful. It is not accidental that in his last work, *An Outline of Psycho-Analysis* (1938), Freud concludes that we still know very little about the mechanisms which underlie the creation of neurotic behavior. Hence psychoanalytic propositions rarely achieve the kind of formal elegance and clarity that mark the standard of philosophic deductions.

The upshot of these three factors is that traditional rationalists, even those sympathetic to the possibility of psychoanalytic truths, will find that Freud is incompatible with their usual values and usual notions of veracity. In most cases the rationalist critic remains a rationalist and Freud is labeled with a current generality (reductionist, hermeneutic theorist, semiotician) and then forgotten. This seems to me wrong.

A final virtue of taking the long road is that we can now read critically the texts on religion with more clarity and less hindrance than otherwise would have been possible. Texts we consider in this final section are "The Uncanny" (1919); *Totem and Taboo* (1912–13), an analysis of primitive religion; *Group Psychology and the Analysis of the Ego* (1921), an analysis of religious leadership and identity; *The Future of an Illusion* (1927), an essay on religious belief; and *Moses and Monotheism* (1939), an imaginative foray into the prehistory of the Jews.

"The Uncanny" (1919)

In this often overlooked yet splendid essay Freud sounds many of the themes on religion proper that he advances in his longer more formal treatises. In keeping with my policy of showing how Freud developed those treatises, and how they are built upon his clinical theory, we examine this essay first. This reflects Freud's general plan of attack. We recall that he began his *Introductory Lectures* by discussing typical and quite unextraordinary behaviors: parapraxes. This rather pretentious term, with its air of scientific obscurity, was not his. It was imported by his English translators. Freud's terms were ordinary German expressions which we might better translate as "mishearing," "missaying," etc. The difference between the two modes of expression is not trivial. It amounts to a difference in point of view: Freud wishes to move from general truths, captured in ordinary language, to the presentation of new truths uncovered by psychoanalysis. His was a general psychology from the beginning. His English translators, like many other academics, began their labors with the wish to demonstrate the power of their discipline and to distinguish it from its competitors. A Freudian approach to religion, then, will first analyze the structure of a universal experience, like that of the uncanny, and then venture onto the analysis of the particular experiences of one group or of one person.

This essay is doubly important to us who wish to evaluate Freud's opinions on religion. First, it carries out his manifest intention to lay the groundwork for the analysis of religion. Second, we see Freud, for the first time, exemplify his own intense ambivalence toward religion.

Technical Terms

Omnipotence of thought

1   Why is Freud obliged to awaken within himself the possibility of experiencing the particular feelings that mark the "uncanny" (p. 220)? What kind of people would not require this effort? Would a perfectly healthy and happy person ever have "uncanny" experiences? (We consider this question at length below.)

2   Reading Freud's accounts of the German term "unheimlich" for the first time may tire one, especially if one is unacquainted with German. One should buck up though and see if his analysis fits the apparently similar English terms, "eery," "weird," "sinister," and "uncanny." An unabridged dictionary will prove an ally. Do these terms designate something that is both known yet unknown and frightening?

3   If there are no strong parallels between the English and German terms, does that fact affect his general argument? Here the good student and good teacher will want to recall as many varied examples of uncanny experiences as possible. In addition to making for a very lively class hour—full of wonderful stories which people are dying to tell—it brings the argument to a point: Why are we so fascinated with fortune telling, ghosts, spirits, ESP, and so on?

4   Following the lead of Jentsch, Freud considers Hoffmann's famous tale about the mechanical doll Olympia whose story evokes a "quite unparalleled atmosphere of uncanniness" (p. 227). Why does Freud say that the key to the story is "ambivalence" rather than "ambiguity"? Why would Hoffmann's faint satire tend to decrease the story's uncanny effect?

5   Consider the nurse's tale about the Sand-Man (the story within the story). Why did she (in contrast to his mother) tell the young boy this story in the first place? Recall our discussion of the Wolf Man's anxieties: Do fairy tales and folklore lend themselves to Freudian interpretation through accident alone? (If fairy tales are full of such

atrocities ought children to be spared them? Would such censorship remove the primary source of children's anxieties?)

6   Freud holds that the source of the tale's particular power is its representation, again and again, of injury to one's eyes. And this he connects to castration anxiety. What is his evidence for this claim? He says that the fear of castration is primary to the fear of damaging one's eyes. Why is this claim so important to his argument? Why would eyes be especially good candidates for symbolic equivalents of the male genitals?

7   The extensive footnote on p. 232 (in the SE) is especially useful for it demonstrates Freud's reconstruction of the original story. What would correspond to it in dream interpretation? What is the father imago and at what psychosexual stage would one expect to find splits like this take place? Given this, why would the theme of castration be repeated so many times in the story—or in a patient's dreams or in his transference fantasies?

8   Consider other uncanny stories (a favorite example is Henry James's *The Turn of the Screw*): Would one expect to find that castration anxiety was always the single most important unconscious element? Both James and Hoffmann employ the theme of doubt on the part of their respective narrators. Given what we know of the genesis of neurotic anxiety (e.g., in the development of the Rat Man's symptoms), why would this ploy be especially likely to succeed? (How is doubt connected to repression and repression to the formation of symptoms?)

9   He turns to the equally fascinating theme of the "double." (Why is this theme fascinating? Is "fascination" akin to "uncanny"?) How is the double linked to "a special faculty" of the mind which is able to oppose the rest of the ego? How is the double connected to the two parts of the father imago? Consider the presence of doubles or side-kicks in popular culture: Do they manifest the latent characteristics Freud predicted of them? (Compare Superman with Don Quixote and Sancho Panza!)

10 He gives more illustrations, including one we have seen already in our discussion of the "Rat Man." Why would obsessional neurotics be especially likely to report uncanny experiences? How is a belief in the "omnipotence of thoughts" (p. 240) manifested in reports of the uncanny? (Consider your own examples of the uncanny taken from everyday life: Do they too manifest a similar belief in the magical power of certain kinds of thoughts?)

11 Freud summarizes his major propositions on p. 241. Explicate his two conclusions and show how each pertains to the "phylogenetic" and "ontogenetic" considerations he advances. Under which rubric should we place the information given us about Hoffmann's

own unhappy boyhood? Assuming that Freud is correct about these two conditions necessary to the production of the uncanny, how might one employ them in the conscious creation of uncanny effects in a film or a novel?

12 "I should not be surprised to hear that psychoanalysis . . . has itself become uncanny to many people for that very reason" (p. 243). Has this occurred? What is the usual understanding of psychoanalysis in our culture? How is it portrayed in the movies, or in *New Yorker* cartoons? Does this occur for any other kind of psychology? Are analysts hated and loved, feared and reviled, like their counterparts in so-called primitive societies?

13 Of the two sources of the uncanny so far discussed, which is most likely to decrease with the advance in civilization and which is most likely to increase? At what point in their treatment would we expect patients undergoing analysis to report uncanny experiences? How might they describe what would appear to be sudden fulfillments of their transference wishes? (Is the uncanny related to the experience known as having chills run up and down one's spine?)

14 ". . . Not everything that recalls repressed desires and surmounted modes of thinking belonging to the prehistory of the individual and of the race—is on that account uncanny" (p. 245). Why not? Why does Freud hesitate to apply his formula to the uncanny in literature in general? What is the peculiarly directive power creative writers exercise over us? Does this mean that the New Testament stories are not fictional—or intended to be read as fiction—since they evoke no uncanny feelings in the reader? Or do they? Is the uncanny a kind of prototypical religious experience?

Totem and Taboo (1912–13)

Preface and Chapter I: The Horror of Incest

Technical Terms

Totem; taboo; categorical imperative; clan; phratry; Haeckel's Law; unconscious sense of guilt; compensation; rituals of excess; vicissitudes; cathexis; projection narcissism of minor differences

1 The preface to this work is vital for there Freud delimits the extent of his claims and inquiry. Why does he feel his comments on taboo are exhaustive while those on totemism are only conjectures? Did Freud do "field work" with regard to either issue? Is psychoanalysis a kind of "anthropology"? If psychoanalytic claims are valid ought they to apply to all people equally?

2　Why does Freud choose to examine the behavior of Australian aborigines, whom he knows only through books, rather than the behavior of groups whom he might have investigated directly? Emile Durkheim, the great French sociologist, studied the same groups in a similar manner at roughly the same time (just before World War I). Why would social theorists in general find the aborigines such attractive subjects?

3　Are concepts like "ancient" and "archaic" applicable to human institutions, like religion, or human behavior, like language? An aborigine living today is as far removed in time from "proto-humans" as we are. How can one say, nevertheless, that the aborigine is "archaic" while we are advanced? (What would characterize an "archaic" language?)

4　After offering definitions of the elusive term "totem," Freud attempts to demonstrate that primitives have an especially great horror of incest. Why is the severity of their punishment for this kind of crime a clue to their fascination and dread of it at the same time? What general psychoanalytic rules is Freud here invoking?

5　It seems one of the most common avoidances is that between son-in-law and mother-in-law. How does Freud connect this fact with the ways in which our culture treats this relationship? Consider three or four examples of this relationship in modern fiction or films. Do they manifest the level of ambivalence implied in Freud's discussion? (An arduous research project suggests itself: to catalogue and analyze all the in-law cartoons that have appeared in the *New Yorker or Playboy* magazines over the last thirty years.)

6　Freud concludes by comparing neurotics, children, and savages (pp. 16–17). Why is this comparison of crucial importance to his general thesis?

Chapter II: Taboo and Emotional Ambivalence

7　Freud says he is much more confident about his interpretation of "taboo" than he is about his interpretation of totemism. Given what we know of his analysis of the "uncanny," why does it follow that "taboo violations have no grounds and are of unknown origin. They are unintelligible to us, to those who are dominated by them . . ." (p. 18)? How will understanding taboo help us understand our own "categorical imperative" (Kant)?

8　According to Wundt (p. 25) earlier stages of mythic thinking are preserved in later stages. What features of neurotic beliefs and actions exemplify a similar preservation? (Consider the three case histories, above: How does each manifest the preservation of archaisms?)

9   In part two of this chapter we are introduced to the psychoanalytic discussion. Given the warning on p. 26 that resemblances need not predict identity, what underlying pattern and what general mechanisms must Freud attribute finally to the creation of taboos if they are to bear a psychoanalytic explanation?

10 The crux of Freud's argument lies in his analogy between obsessional neurotic patterns and taboo practices. Analyze both the Maori chief example and the Mrs. Smith example (p. 28). (See p. 96 after trying your hand.) Fill in the latter account with a conjecture as to the likely reason Mrs. Smith has become "taboo." (Note the prohibition upon touching suggested in the final sentence in the paragraph.)

11 One of the more puzzling aspects of "taboo illness" is the speed and dexterity with which the target of the prohibitions changes (e.g., recall Rat Man's intricate and contorted prayers). Why does Freud argue that these instances of displacement are exact indicators of the fact of repression? Why does it make no sense to ask savages for the reason behind their taboo practices?

12 Freud formulates quickly the two essential "laws" of totemism. Of what central psychosexual conflict are they the obvious and complete correlates? Must each member of the group share the unconscious desires against which these laws are erected? Why must a primitive group, especially, inflict upon transgressors of these rules such severe punishment? How are taboo violators treated in our culture—are they criminals or "sick"?

13 In parts three and four of this chapter Freud sets out to argue that the formal similarities between taboo and obsessional illness are more than happenstance. Why is he so keen upon demonstrating that both are the results of primal ambivalence? How does he show this for rites? Consider his examples of taboo restrictions upon the treatment of enemies, the dead, and chiefs. Are there any similar restrictions—together with rituals of excess—in our culture? (Why are newly installed American presidents granted a "honeymoon" period, as the media cliche has it? What usually happens on a honeymoon? Why are honeymoons called honeymoons?)

14 Rituals of mourning and rites of interment are fascinating topics for psychoanalytic research since so much of the analysis of a normal person includes uncovering a whole slew of death wishes against loved ones and others. The observation and analysis of a typical funeral rite in our culture, together with a careful reading of Freud's great essay "Mourning and Melancholia" (1917, SE 14), would make an excellent field assignment. (On mourning and the fear of demons see Freud's remarks in section four, p. 65.)

15 How is it that neurotics are atavistic vestiges of our primitive

ancestors? Does this mean that there is a phylogenetic, that is, inherited, tendency toward regression operating in people prone to neurosis? How might one go about measuring such a tendency? Yet most people are not neurotics. Does it follow that there is, therefore, no connection between their sense of guilt (or wrong) and what appears to be our common ancestry? (Do modern American religious practices and teaching encourage or discourage the formation of a sense of guilt?)

16 ". . . There is no need to prohibit something that no one desires to do, and a thing that is forbidden with the greatest emphasis must be a thing that is desired" (p. 69). Why is this claim crucial to Freud's entire argument? Is it plausible? (See also p. 123.) Consider four or five things American children are forbidden to do, as well as four or five prohibitions from other groups: Do they manifest a similar structure? (Note that they must be actions which are taboo, not merely dangerous or costly, e.g., a child is forbidden to carve the dining room table because it ruins a costly piece of furniture.)

An equally interesting field of inquiry is the immense number of taboos established around race relations in multiracial societies, e.g., the American South, South Africa, and most South American countries with sizable European populations. If what is tabooed is what is naturally, but unconsciously, desired, what might we conjecture about the psychological source of institutionalized racism? How could one begin this kind of investigation?

17 Freud concludes this long chapter with a famous comparison between three great social institutions and three types of neuroses. Why are the latter asocial structures (note the Norton paperback edition dropped the 'a' from asocial)? Each line of these final two paragraphs is a condensed (and brilliant) assertion and is worthy of intense reflection. For example, why is it that sexual needs do not unite "men" in the same way as egoistic (or self-preservative) ones? (Related issues are raised in Bonner, 1980; Wilson, 1975; and Wilson and Lumsden, 1981.)

Chapter III: Animism, Magic, and Omnipotence of Thoughts

18 It is fashionable to explain Freud's opinions on religion and his theory of primitive religion, especially, as reflections of his 19th-century milieu, one of evolutionary speculation, racist doctrines masquerading as science, and so on. In what ways is he guilty of these charges—given, for example, his thesis about the three great stages in human evolution (p. 77)? How might one go about measuring the change or alternation in group consciousness between, say,

the Greeks and the present day? Must evolution coincide with history? If so, does it follow that medieval science and religion and philosophy were of a much higher "stage" than those of the Athenian Greeks?

19 After summarizing the opinions of the experts of his day, especially those of Frazer, Freud says they overlooked the "dynamic" factor (p. 83). What is a dynamic factor—in psychoanalytic terms? How does the Rat Man's phrase "the omnipotence of thoughts" aid Freud in arguing that there is a continuum between primitive magic, modern prayers, children's games, and our common dream life? How is each a "vicissitude" of this universal belief?

20 Freud invokes his libido theory to account for this universal phenomenon. Why is "overvaluation" a key element in his argument? What in the world is "narcissistic cathexis"? As always, one cannot understand these kinds of abstract psychoanalytic formulations without having examined a goodly number of examples. So get four or five examples of narcissistic cathexis: Ought they to be related to the famous oral, anal, phallic triad? (Can a teenage boy sometimes love his car like he loves his parents or himself?)

21 Is Freud disdainful of the savages about whom he is writing? Nineteenth-century authorities on primitives explained most of their behavior as irrationally motivated. What is wrong with this approach—according to Freud? Would a group retain expensive and arduous rituals, like those described on p. 98, if they had no adaptive value? Must a group or society recognize those values? Might it prove more advantageous for them to sacralize and mystify the rationale for their actions? Why is marital fidelity, for example, so crucial to our society? How is it enforced?

IV: The Return of Totemism in Childhood

22 Consider the footnote on pp. 102–103 and Freud's assessment of the reliability of his sources and, consequently, of the reliability of his own conjectures. Is it more difficult to understand children than adults? What kind of people seem especially "good" with children? Can one acquire these kinds of talents? Would psychoanalytic psychotherapy, in principle, help one in that endeavor?

23 After quoting Reinach's *code du totemisme*, Freud enumerates conflicting theories about the origin of this apparently universal cultural institution. Why is he especially intent upon arguing that totemism and exogamy are necessarily linked together (pp. 120–125)? Freud wants to show that the horror of incest is inherited but not instinctual—what is the difference between the two modes of transmission of behavior? What kinds of additional experimental

evidence would help one choose between them?

24   What is the "return of totemism" in childhood? Why did Little
      Arpad say that he would like to eat "some fricasse of mother"
      (p. 131)? Is this a normal appetite for a young boy? How does
      Freud go from the analysis of his and Little Hans's phobias to
      claiming that the totemic animal is but a substitute for the father?

25   In part four of this final chapter, Freud leans upon the work of
      Robertson-Smith (whose book is fascinating, by the way). Why
      would some guests of Bedouin's be sure and part company after
      they have shared a meal, but before making a prolonged excur-
      sion to the bathroom?

26   Having summarized and transformed Robertson-Smith's theory,
      in part four, Freud marries it to Darwin's speculations about the
      origin of human social groups, in part five. What is the fantastic
      hypothesis born of this union? In a note on p. 142 Freud refers to
      evidence that mammalian herds often manifest a kind of horde
      structure, in which a dominant male controls sexual access to the
      females. Is this relevant to his speculations about the origin of
      primal groups? If so, ought we to find vestiges of the same feel-
      ings and attitudes in modern peoples? And do we? (Does Freud?)

27   Given the analysis of totemic religion, e.g., on p. 145, is it fair to
      conclude that it, as well as later variations of it, are overdeter-
      mined? If so, what characteristics must we expect to find associ-
      ated with it? Is there any form of a totemic sacrifice in Christian
      or Jewish religious traditions? (Why is Jesus called the Lamb of
      God? How does He take away the sins of the world?)

28   If the totem animal (or symbol which stands for the animal) rep-
      resents the father and the god-head also represents the father,
      why this double representation? Recall the Rat Man's feelings
      about his father: Do you find in that story splits in the father-
      imago similar to those occurring in Christianity? How did the
      "father-religion" become a "son-religion", and why does Freud
      feel this is a key to understanding the triumph of Christianity,
      especially in the West? (Would this also help account for the deep
      animosity official Christianity has shown towards Judaism?)

29   Freud concludes this grand synthesis by suggesting that one can-
      not account for the persistence of primal ambivalence and the
      sense of guilt without assuming that mental characteristics are
      somehow inherited. Is this a plausible Darwinian claim? If not,
      must it be incorrect?

30   He refers to Goethe's anti-Christian masterpiece. Why does he use
      this quotation in this final statement? To which Old Testament and
      New Testament verses does Goethe's line refer? Finally, does it fol-
      low that neurotics cannot make use of those cultural institutions,

including religion, which deal with the primal wishes (and memories) that underlie their own disorder? And if this is true, can one properly say that ordinary religion, that is, religion amenable to and established within a culture, is neurotic?

Group Psychology and the Analysis of the Ego (1921)

I: Introduction

This essay, which Freud had begun drafting in 1919, is usually overlooked in standard accounts of Freud's psychology of religion. Although there is a short chapter on the Catholic Church, it is perfunctory and no more extensive than a similar discussion of social hierarchy within the army. Yet the essay as a whole is vital for it illustrates the ways in which Freud sought to develop his theory of the person into a theory of the group. More so, it entails Freud's most powerful theoretical critique of religion.

1 Freud feels he has to demonstrate that he has some right to speak of "group psychology," and he proffers an argument to that effect in this first section. What distinguishes "social phenomena," in this text, from those he wishes to term "narcissistic"? Although we do not read *The Ego and the Id* (1923) in our common labor, a fuller understanding of his claims will be gained by considering his famous notion of the superego (see below, chapter eight). Why does it make sense to say that the superego is a "social phenomenon"?

2 Recall Freud's comparison of the neuroses with social institutions: neurotics, he said, had turned away from social reality, and sought refuge in their fantasies. Is this consistent with his claim, in this text, that sociologists and group psychologists have argued for a "social instinct" that might better be described as the outgrowth of individual instincts operating within a small group, the family? (He mentions the individual's relationship to the physician—what other name might we attach to this relationship? Could transference occur at a "distance"?)

II: Le Bon's Description of the Group Mind

3 Just as he used anthropological authorities in *Totem and Taboo*, both as sources of information and as foils against which he could present his own thinking, Freud here uses Le Bon's famous discussion of "groups" (which includes what we would term "mobs") to set off his own theory. What are the three questions Freud asserts a complete theory ought to answer, and why is it best to begin with the third? Why is the question of the "bonding agent" so important to Freud?

4   Le Bon appears to have a dynamic theory of group formation for he too speaks about the "unconscious" elements that emerge when individuals enter into a group and throw off what was unique to them. Does Freud share this view? Is Le Bon's notion of the "unconscious" more compatible with Jung's, for example? A popular image of Freud's notion of the "unconscious" is that it contains all that is worst in human feelings and wishes, hence, what is "repressed," that is, forced into this dynamic unconscious, is always evil and vicious. But is this true? What kinds of feelings and wishes did Dora, Rat Man, and Wolf Man repress? Could someone repress wishes that were in themselves innocent and even loving?

5   Why does Le Bon use the notion of "suggestion" in his explanation of group formation? How do most novelists, movie directors, TV authors, etc., picture the status of an individual caught up in a group? How do they tend to portray mobs, strikes, and other mass movements? In other words, do they subscribe to Le Bon's theory or to Freud's?

6   It will be useful to outline Le Bon's assessment of the characteristics of groups: Do they have any positive features? How do college football crowds, for example, treat the opposing players—especially after having lost the "big game"? Who, according to Freud, makes the great decisions and momentous discoveries that advance our civilization? In fact, what is the very worst failing Freud attributes to groups? Do you agree?

7   As is often true, it pays to read Freud's footnotes, like that on p. 79. Why can a child tolerate the presence of two wholly incompatible feelings about a parent, for example, while an adult could not? How is the gradual coordination of the sexual instincts parallel to the gradual consolidation of the ego? Give an example or two from any of the three case histories in which the patient tolerated a "split" in his or her ego for some time, but finally reacted, "with all the usual consequences" (p. 79).

8   Are Le Bon's notion of "prestige" (p. 81), Freud's notion of "transference," and Max Weber's notion of "charisma" similar to one another? (Weber's famous concept is discussed in his *The Sociology of Religion.*) Are they compatible with one another?

III: Other Accounts of Collective Mental Life

9   After praising Le Bon's work and adopting his descriptions, Freud appears to take it all back in this chapter when he points out a major contradiction in Le Bon's account. How does the fact of language (p. 83), for example, argue against an entirely negative assessment of groups? Considering Freud's analysis of the uncanny in the essay

by that name, why would he be especially concerned to praise the "power" and "genius" of natural languages, like German and English? Does dream interpretation itself require one to know and use the genius of language? How so?

10 Why does Freud bother to quote from McDougall, whose opinions on the nature of a group appear as incorrect and ordinary as those of Le Bon? Why is the problem of "raising collective mental life to a higher level" (p. 86) so important? How do both Freud and McDougall picture the qualities of an individual who is not enmeshed in the workings of a "primitive group"?

IV: Suggestion and Libido

11 Freud refers to a number of authorities who attempted to explain how a group is able to influence an individual, usually for the worse. Chief among their theories is the notion of "suggestion." How does this theory, in the midst of a psychotherapeutic encounter, sometimes lead to "violence" (p. 89)? Why does Freud quote the riddle about Christopher? Has this notion been retained in social scientific work after Freud? (What unconscious fantasies might likely be aroused by the notion of suggestion should a therapist introduce it into the treatment relationship?)

12 Not too surprisingly Freud argues that "libido" is a better concept and ought to replace "suggestion." Why? What central characteristic of libidinal activities make "libido" a better (more scientific and more concrete) term for explaining the formation of groups? (See his comments on Trotter, p. 87.) In the numerous treatises on "Love" one finds the author typically attempts to distinguish between types of love (sexual, friendship, parental, divine, etc.). C. S. Lewis's book, *The Four Loves* (1960) is one such example, though written at a level and with a skill much beyond the average. What's wrong with these books in general? Why does Freud, again, turn to the "genius" of language in order to help justify his unitarian conception of "libido"?

13 Reflecting back upon our reading of the three case histories, does one find that Dora, for example, had radically different concepts of love? For example, did she distinguish between her feelings for Herr K, for her father and for Freud? If there are no fundamental differences between these types of feelings, how can a child, for example, learn to distinguish "appropriate" from "inappropriate" behavior? Consider Freud's remarks on the formation and dissolution of the Rat Man's feelings about his father.

14 "Let us remember that the authorities make no mention of any such [erotic] relations" (p. 91). Why is this not sufficient evidence

that these relations are not in fact erotic?

V: Two Artificial Groups: The Church and the Army

15 "A church and an army are artificial groups . . ." (p. 93). Why? Is punishment an important element in the creation and maintenance of most religious organizations? How is discipline enforced? With what other kinds of groups is Freud comparing these two? Why does he say that both church and army are held together by an illusion of love? Why use the term "illusion" in this context?

16 Do all great leaders, whether ethical or not, at least pretend to feel a compassion and affection for their followers? Is this true of American political leaders as well? (Consider FDR's fireside chats.) How could a wiser German General Staff have helped prevent the destruction of Wilson's 14 points? (Was Wilson an idealist who also failed to see the importance of illusion?)

17 How does Freud use the existence of panic to argue against McDougall's "rationalistic" explanation? Under what conditions does one find that panic spreads like a contagion? Why would the breaking of emotional ties lead to a state of panic in otherwise well-disciplined troops? If Freud is correct, what illusion would the clever leader always hope to convey about his or her feelings toward each of his followers?

18 He continues his analysis of panic with reference to a popular novel of his time. Why would such a story enjoy "extremely large sales" (p. 98)? Would it in our time too? And what shall we say of his assessment of the nature of the religion of love? Must it be necessarily hard and unloving to outsiders? Why? How does Freud explain the decrease in wars of religion and religious persecutions? Because we are better people in whom reason now reigns supreme?

VI: Further Problems and Lines of Work

19 Which of the two great emotions, love and hate, is primary and which is secondary? Why would Freud find this question inappropriate and misbegotten? Of the two great loves, love of self and love of others, which is primary and which is secondary? Is it just Europeans who manifest a narcissism of minor differences? What kind of libido is, as it were, the fuel or energy source to which groups have access and with which they carry out their enterprises? Do you find Freud's basic contentions supported or contradicted by the techniques fund raisers and politicians employ? Why do candidates wear Indian hats on reservations and hard hats in union halls?

20 What does "desexualized, sublimated homosexual love for other men" (p. 103) mean? Would most men accept this description of their motives for remaining within group formations? Would they recognize any truth at all in this metapsychological formulation? Freud realizes that his propositions will fail to convince most of us. Yet they have the merit of leading us to consider a more fundamental issue: identification.

VII: Identification

21 This is an extremely important chapter, even though it is only six pages. It is also extremely misleading. For example, the first sentence is not true, according to other things Freud has told us, since we must assume that infants manifest emotional ties with others prior to the development of classical oedipal feelings. (On this point see Schafer [1968] in which he elaborates the differences between identification, assimilation and introjection.) What central tendency of mental life and ego development is responsible for the creation of the oedipal *complex*?

22 Freud appears to say that the boy's competition with his father for his mother's favor causes him to hate the old man: but is this so? Why does he invoke the case of the cannibal at this juncture? Which features of the Rat Man's story manifest similar cannibalistic features? And which elements in "Dora" are also similar?

23 Freud tries to distinguish between wanting to be like one's father and wanting to have one's father as a sexual object. Which is the more mature desire? Is this a linguistic distinction merely? Can we count on the genius of natural languages to come to Freud's rescue as it has in the past? The SE translators use the term "ego" on these pages (pp. 106–107) when referring to a person. Are there better terms? What type of persons and which age groups seem especially prone to imitate people whom they respect or admire? If a patient like Dora begins to imitate the analyst, is that a sign that she is advancing along the paths of ego maturation? Why would group identifications of the kind described on p. 107 contribute to repression? Given this claim, how would Freud assess the utility of group psychotherapy in general?

24 Does Freud denigrate those who manifest identification? Ought psychoanalysts and others in helping professions to display "empathy"? Is Freud correct in not distinguishing empathy from sympathy? Was he empathic with Dora, in your judgment? Are there general characteristics that empathic persons share? Are your best teachers empathic—must they be so? What virtues might an empathic teacher exhibit and what role might such teachers play

in the development of one's emotional life (p. 108)?

25 Freud then discusses two additional examples of identification: that which he says is present in some kinds of homosexuality and that which appears in some cases of melancholia (note the two essays to which he refers in the footnote on p. 109). What does the phrase "it remoulds the ego in one of its important features—in its sexual character—upon the model of what has hitherto been the object" (pp. 108–109) mean? How is he using the term "ego" here? Ought one to find this kind of identification in all cases of homosexuality? How does identification preserve the lost object in both cases?

26 In an especially laconic sentence he describes how identification is a first step in the creation of both melancholia and other behaviors in which conscience rages against part of the self. Is this persuasive? Consider an example of the workings of conscience in any one of the three case histories we discussed above. Why is conscience so often associated with a voice? Where does the voice come from and to whom does it belong? In other words, whose voice was it originally? Why is there no eye of conscience? (And why are there evil eyes but not evil voices?)

27 He ascribes a number of functions to an agency here termed the ego-ideal. (Note that these functions are not those Freud will later attribute to the agency he terms the superego in his 1923 text, *The Ego and the Id.*) Is the differentiation between ego and ego-ideal an automatic event that occurs necessarily at a fixed time and in a fixed mode in all people? Does it serve or hinder the aims of civilization? Would successful psychoanalytic treatment enhance or reduce one's tendency toward this differentiation? (How might the analytic situation itself, in which the therapist sits behind the patient, contribute to the construction of a more differentiated ego-ideal? Are there corresponding arrangements in traditional religious practices?)

VIII: Being in Love and Hypnosis

28 As we have seen repeatedly, Freud appeals to the genius of ordinary language (rather than to the technical terms of science) when he launches a new generalization about psychic life (cf. his reliance upon the testimony of great artists whom he claims corroborate his theories). Why and how does he rely upon the ordinary uses of the word "love"? (Children say they love ice cream, their parents correct them and have them say instead that they "like" ice cream. With whom does Freud side?)

29 Sexual love is famous for its intense and short-lived qualities. Upon

orgasm either sleep or boredom prevail. Yet Freud unabashedly claims that it is sexual love which animates us, even to the carrying out of lengthy labors the ends of which one may not envision, or if envisioned, may not reach. What guarantees the possibility of maintaining a lasting cathexis? Given this general theorem, which is unhappily buried in this, why would neurotic symptoms manifest a repetitious (cyclical) nature?

30 How does the multiphasic structure of libidinal development contribute to the elaboration of erotic variations like "affection"? Surely most adolescents, for example, would deny that their feelings for their parents are sexual. Are they wrong? Were Dora's feelings for her father sexual—only? Under what circumstances might one find affection turning back into sexual feelings? What kinds of transformations—in horror films, for example—seem especially fascinating to an audience (to us)? How do groups treat a fallen hero, say a basketball player, who fails to maintain his ideal status?

31 ". . . We have always been struck by the phenomenon of sexual overvaluation . . ." (p. 112). Why is overvaluation a sure sign that the lover has found in the beloved a vehicle which bears the original store of narcissism? Is it true, by the way, that adolescent love is an activity carried out as if the lover wore blinders? Is love blind? Who, according to new parents, has the most beautiful baby in the world? Whose school is the greatest and whose father is the strongest in the world?

32 Yet, according to Freud in this chapter, the idealization of the beloved cannot proceed if there is too much satisfaction. Why? If this is so, how might Freud explain the standard Western (civilized) requirements of chastity before marriage and fidelity afterwards? Are these still ideals to which the majority would ascribe? When do we know that idealization has gone too far?

33 Freud goes on to make an especially obscure distinction: an object may replace either the ego or the ego ideal (p. 114). This gives him a way to show how hypnosis—one of the mysteries of the 19th century and about which he wrote a great deal—is similar to being in love. How are they alike? If, as the footnote tells us, Freud later changed his mind and attributed reality testing to the ego, does the analogy still hold? Why is hypnosis *not* a good analogy for group formation? (Is hypnosis an uncanny topic for most people too?)

34 Having said why he finds hypnosis an unattractive model of group formation (just as he had earlier rejected it as a mode of psychotherapy), Freud offers us one of his rare charts (p. 116). (He provides graphic representations of his model of the mind in *SE* 5, pp. 537–541; *SE* 19, p. 24; and *SE* 22, p. 70 as well). Most people

find this diagram exceedingly obscure. A hint as to its meaning may lie in the next to last sentence, the one in italic letters. Note that the arrows go from right (the external object) to left (the ego ideal). In so doing they pass from the external world (where the ideal persists) to the internal world (where each individual maintains a representation of it). The vertical, dotted lines that run down from the ego ideal and ego would seem to represent the unification of individuals, first via their common ideal and, secondly, via their common ego identity. They represent the linchpins, as it were, without which the group would fly apart.

IX: The Herd Instinct

35   In the first paragraph of this chapter Freud seems to admit that his speculations on the formation of groups have led us only to more questions. Yet in the second paragraph he states—as if it had been demonstrated—that "regression" is an essential characteristic of groups. How did he manufacture this crucial theorem out of the doubt he advanced initially? Where else have we seen the equation of neuroses, infantile behaviors, and group processes?

36   After praising Trotter's description of the herd instinct, Freud takes him to task for overlooking the question of ontogenesis (p. 119). Why? Why does Freud argue that the "group" mind cannot be a primary entity, and that, on the contrary, it is derived from the child's earliest struggles? Given this analysis why do older children come to love younger ones about whose welfare they are especially solicitous?

37   What is Freud's recipe for the creation of the group ideal of equal justice for all and all for one and one for all? Why does he use the term "reaction-formation" (p. 120)? Having worked through a number of his major texts we should be able to predict which kinds of feelings and which objects will be subject to this form of defense: and which are those? Under what conditions would one expect to see reaction-formations "dissolve"? (Which of the three patients, Dora, Rat Man, or Wolf Man, exhibited the most pronounced instances of reaction formation?) Why might persons who are religiously devout tend to be particularly marked by an excess of reaction formations?

38   Freud refers to the famous story about King Solomon who was asked to adjudicate a dispute in which two women, one of whom had just lost her child, claimed to be the mother of the same child. Consider Solomon's wisdom in offering to divide the disputed child in half: How is this story interpreted normally, and how does Freud's interpretation differ?

39 Has Freud been persuaded by anything that Trotter or Le Bon has proposed? If so, name those factors. If not, why has he bothered to refer to them at all? Do groups always require the presence of an esteemed leader who loves all equally? How do groups respond to leaders who appear to favor one member over the others? Why should rock stars, charismatic leaders, and popular teachers be particularly cautious about charges of favoritism? (That these kinds of persons are the recipients of primary narcissism is shown by what essential fact in their fans' behavior?)

X: The Group and the Primal Horde

40 Which is older: the individual as we understand him or her to exist in our culture or the group? If Freud's answer is the correct one why would it follow that innovative thinking, particularly science as we know it, could *not* arise in group contexts? And how is this event in turn linked to the existence of private property? (Recall Freud's opinions on the source of great discoveries, above.) Why is it more correct to say, according to Freud, that there are and always have been two distinct psychological types? Is Nietzsche's "superman" identical to the great leader that Freud describes? (How did Nietzsche portray the life of great heroes prior to the civilization of the West by the forces of Christianity?)

41 Freud then recaps his general story about the origins of the group and the primal father's response to his sons. Is there any science or any mode of research the practitioners of which could verify these claims? Note: Why does Freud mention the honeybee example (p. 124)? If anthropologists and primatologists showed conclusively that protohumans never manifested primal horde behavior, would or could Freud maintain his general theory of group psychology? Would he be able to retain his general theory of the origins of religion too?

42 How did the lack of inhibitions upon his sexual urges lead the original primal father to exhibit an unbridled narcissism? Is this evident today? How do gossip magazines and similar periodicals portray the sexual life of movie stars and other heroes? And is the public equally willing to allow university deans and business leaders a similar range of sexual highjinks? If not, what may we conclude about our general understanding of the degree to which such community leaders may exhibit narcissistic behaviors? Can a politician ever be anything other than humble and grateful for the chance of serving this nation?

43 One cannot look upon the face of the godhead, according to Freud's reading of the stories about Moses, without fear and

dread. Is this a general feature of the great world religions? With what kind of light does a person's face shine—according to Freud's psychoanalytic explanation? Consider expressions like "beaming approval," "a show of pride," "eyes shining approval," etc. The biblical story explains the light showing in Moses' face as a transferral of manna; how must we understand it? How would you characterize the faces of young women, for example, watching their favorite musician perform on stage?

44   Although he does not employ the concept of hypnosis in his theory, Freud allows that ordinary language is not wrong when it speaks of an especially powerful person as hypnotic. Why is ordinary language correct here too? Is hypnosis an uncanny topic in our times? Consider the footnote on p. 126 (about the transference): Would a hypnotic method increase or decrease the likelihood of insight? Would hypnotic treatment require more or less work than that required by psychoanalysis? Finally, which is primary: the phenomenon of hypnosis or unchecked narcissism?

XI: A Differentiating Grade in the Ego

This is another especially condensed chapter. It contains one of Freud's most succinct expressions on the relationship between the individual and society. One way to underscore its central question is to ask: How does the selfish infant become a self-sacrificing adult? In other words, how is primary narcissism transformed into the love of others: How is sacrificial love forged out of the raw materials of instinctual love of self?

45   In the first paragraph Freud summarizes the work up to this point. What is the "prodigy" he mentions in the last sentence of this paragraph and again in the first sentence of the second? (Why would he use a term like this—where else have we seen him emphasize the extraordinary nature of a phenomenon everyone else takes for granted?)

46   What can Freud mean by the phrase "more freedom of libido" (p. 129)? If Freud is correct in his general understanding of the formation of groups, under what conditions would one expect to find that the incidence of mass behaviors, including the formation of charismatic groups, increases (p. 129)? How can it be that many people become great leaders because their followers make them great? Give an illustration of such an event: Would the followers in such an event be aware of their part in the creation of their hero? *Could* they become aware? How might they respond to someone like Freud informing them of their roles in the manufacture of charisma?

47   The sentence on p. 130 beginning "Each of the mental differenti-
      ations that we have become acquainted with" states Freud's fun-
      damental theorem about the ego. What universal psychological
      phenomenon exemplifies this return to a "self-sufficient narcis-
      sism"? If this fundamental theorem is correct, which type of peo-
      ple are most susceptible to the breakdown of the ego? And which
      are least? Why must the ego be "maintained"? How do jokes,
      humor, and other cultural forms contribute to that task? How
      might we explain the rise of psychoanalysis at the end of the 19th
      century (a century in which official religion no longer dominated
      every aspect of the intellectual world and political realm)?

48   As often happens in Freud, he breaks off his exposition, particularly
      in these more technical papers, to take up themes developed else-
      where. This is especially true of his remarks on narcissism, which he
      set out most completely in his 1914 paper (in SE 14). A thorough
      explication of his thoughts on religion would include a close reading
      of that essay. However, lacking the time and space necessary for
      carrying out that effort, we can still ask: How prevalent are issues of
      narcissism in ordinary religion? Does petitionary prayer, for exam-
      ple, reveal a narcissistic structure? Do other forms of worship mani-
      fest a similar configuration? Are there any religious institutions that
      do not manifest a concern for or transformation of narcissistic
      wishes and needs?

49   Freud breaks off his exposition, again, to take up the problem of
      manic-depressive illness (pp. 131–133). Is he sure that every case of
      this type of mental disease is caused solely by psychogenic factors?
      Why does identification of the ego with the ego-ideal produce ela-
      tion while the failure of identification produces either shame or
      guilt? Consider a handful of hymns or other devotional aids: What
      kinds of feelings do they tend to induce in the faithful? Do they
      produce feelings of joy and pleasure? And are these two feelings the
      same as mania? If not, is Freud correct about the emotion which
      unification of ego and ego-ideal creates? Are religious joy and reli-
      gious pleasure sublimated forms of mania? Did the Wolf Man gain
      any pleasure out of his boyish religious practices?

XII: Postscript

50   Although there are few authors who have his rhetorical power
      Freud rarely gives one the impression that he has come to a final
      and complete understanding of the subject matter under considera-
      tion. (Is this true of theological treatises in general?) In note A he
      distinguishes between two forms of identification. Does he agree
      with the Christian claim that the church demands a form of ethical

labor higher than that of the primal horde? Is the church, then, more than a group? How?

51 Alfred Kroeber, a famous American anthropologist, has called Freud's theory of the primal horde, here repeated, a just-so story. Does Freud agree? Just-so stories are types of fairy tales—and does Freud believe that the latter are themselves nothing more than pleasant fictions? How does he understand the role of the original poet—were his songs merely entertaining divertisements? Or were they something else? Recall the conclusion to *Totem and Taboo*: Why was the deed prior to the word (or to the song)? Is the hero myth a lie (p. 137) and nothing else?

52 In part C, Freud summarizes his basic theory of the development of adult, aim-inhibited, passions. Which appears first: sexual longing or affection? Even if it is true that children are particularly erotic creatures, unembarrassed about their bodies and unencumbered with prudery, why must we conclude that adult forms of affection are nothing but "sublimated" forms of those earlier sexual longings? Why cannot one form fade away and be replaced by a later, more mature form? How did the primal father contribute to his sons' capacity to sublimate their original sexual and aggressive impulses?

53 He carries out this analysis in the next section. Is it true that there is no room for heterosexual love within the two great institutions he names? Why would a wise leader require celibacy of those whose task it was to create (through their labor) an institution which, like the Roman Catholic Church, requires sacrifice of both clergy and laity? In other words, how does celibacy contribute to the construction of a cultural institution? If this is so, why does it follow that sexual love between a man and a woman is particularly dangerous to a rigid institution? (Up until the last decade most universities forbade departments from appointing a married couple to their staff. Why would this seem to be a good rule to so many administrators?)

54 How are philosophico-religious sects and the like "crooked cures" for all kinds of neurosis? Would any one of the three patients with whom we are now familiar have joined a mystical sect? Why do people join such sects? Under what economic and social circumstances does the number of such sects appear to increase? (For a wonderful description of some 19th-century American sects see William James's classic text, *The Varieties of Religious Experience* [1902].)

55 Finally, he concludes by summarizing the developmental series that extends from being in love to the formation of groups, like the church. Are any of these states—being in love, hypnosis, and the formation of the group—completely primitive? Why do the

neuroses stand outside this developmental sequence? Why does the period of latency become a complicating factor in human development? Recall the general developmental histories of the three patients whose stories we have read. Does each of them show both (1) a period of latency, and (2) an increase in mental conflict following that period? If Freud is correct about the central role latency plays in human development, how ought a well-developed tradition, like that of the Catholic church, to treat children during this period? What kinds of ritual, for example, might we expect the church to require of latency age girls?

The Future of an Illusion (1927)

Technical Terms

Illusion; frustration; prohibition; privation; mental wealth; humanization of nature; hallucination; delusion

Chapter I

1   Freud sets the tone and problem for the entire book in this first paragraph. The tone is worth comparing to that of the clinical essays. What is the difference? Do the first and last sentences in the paragraph mesh together in a coherent way? Is anything left out of Freud's description of the problem of time? Are the sentences in the first two paragraphs of a different length than comparable sentences in the other texts we have read? If so, how would you account for this difference?

2   The SE editor tells us the German term, "Kultur," which Freud uses in his title and in another famous essay, "Civilization and Its Discontents" (1930), may mean either civilization or culture. Freud is aware of the distinction yet he says he scorns it (p. 6). Why? Why would he find this usual distinction contrary to his major developmental theses? He then describes three factors that mark the two aspects of the relationship between civilization and the individual. Which of these three is a particularly Freudian claim?

3   Why is it natural to suppose that the struggles between the aims of civilization and those of the individual are not inherent (p. 6)? Is this not a plausible philosophic opinion? We see Freud return to the theme of work: What dynamic principle, illustrated numerous times in the three case histories, guarantees that all civilizations will deny this basic truth of their origins? If this is so, how would official spokespersons respond to Freud's argument? (Freud refers to this principle indirectly on p. 8 where he summarizes the two great shortcomings of the masses.)

4   Freud never abandoned his 19th-century conviction that the
    world of ultimate reality was the physical world. If this is so, and
    if civilizations or societies "run" on some kind of energy, from
    what sources must they secure it? Why can we not place too
    much hope in the idea that each new generation may further the
    aims of civilization and so slowly advance the work of culture?

5   Could not psychoanalysis itself contribute to this great task? If the
    answer to this question is yes, ought one to find that children of
    psychoanalysts, for example, are both more emotionally developed
    and intellectually freer than the majority? And is this so? Freud
    would appear to be less modest in this essay than he was in *Group
    Psychology* where he averred his lack of expertise. What elements
    in his science and life's work give him a firsthand knowledge about
    the struggle between the individual and his or her culture?

Chapter II

6   What are "the rebelliousness and destructive mania of the partici-
    pants in civilization" (p. 10)? Where else have we seen Freud use
    the term mania? If a person or a group is capable of mania, what
    must we conclude about their unconscious wishes and their con-
    scious fears? At the end of the previous chapter Freud had
    referred indirectly to the Soviet experiment with a universal
    application of Marxist principles. Is he optimistic or pessimistic
    about their chances at building a free and just society in which
    there is no coercion?

7   Beginning at least with Alfred Adler many brilliant students of
    psychoanalysis have attempted to marry it to Marxist theory. Why
    would this appear to be a good match? Is it, though? Which ele-
    ments in Freud's social theory would one have to reject in order
    to wed the two? This is another way of asking if Freud's social
    theory, as articulated in this book and others of this period, is
    grounded upon his clinical theory. And is it?

8   Have we "slipped unawares out of the economic field into the
    field of psychology" (p. 10)? Yet it appears that the species has
    changed, for the better, if we look back to the practices of
    savages. Surely this means that we can look forward to similar
    advances in the species? Does Freud deny, entirely, the validity of
    either claim? Why is it only to the non-psychoanalytic eye that
    cannibalism appears to have been surmounted? (What feelings do
    tales about cannibalism evoke in most people in our times? In
    which cultural fields do we find cannibalism alive and well?)

9   Why does Freud say that internalization is the psychological pro-
    cess most important to the development of civilization? Recall our

discussion of the process of identification as Freud described it in *Group Psychology*: Could a society ever reach a stage in which it was no longer necessary to suppress or otherwise control cannibalistic wishes? Why might one say that even the most sublime forms of religious thought, like that about the Holy Spirit, cannot abandon a reliance upon archaic forms of internalization?

10 While there has been a kind of progress in the civilization of oedipal wishes, for example, other forms of human fault persist (pp. 11–12). Why is Freud so sure of this claim? On what grounds and with what evidence could he support this contention? (Recall the unconscious wishes and beliefs catalogued in the three case histories. Is it only people like Dora whom we would expect to find enmeshed in such tainted ideas?)

11 Yet culture has a way of paying one back for the severe taxation it levies against everyone. What are these ways? Are they payment in full, or are they debased in some manner? Is it with hard currency or inflated currency that one's civilization repays us for our labor, including our libidinal sacrifices? Who, in contemporary American society, appears most gratified by patriotic displays and which groups seem least involved and least emotionally attached to them? Do both kinds of groups take part in the "most important item in the psychical inventory of a civilization" (p. 14)?

Chapter III

12 Why does Freud begin this chapter with this question and why does he use the word peculiar? Has he demonstrated that religious ideas are peculiar? From this dramatic question he leaps to another precipice upon which he balances the archaic unconscious against the claims of civilization. Would the condition he describes lead to a state of splendid enjoyment? There have been episodes, like those of the Nazi death camps, where one group had total authority over the lives of members of another. Were members of the first group splendidly happy?

13 But there are other moments when, Freud says, one gains an exalting impression of the work of mankind. What typifies these situations? Do you find a similar sentiment in fairy tales, or myths, or in movie films? (Is nature majestic, cruel and inexorable? Why is she a "she"? Do all or most cultures picture nature as a feminine force? If yes, how might Freud account for this uniformity? How is this general propensity related to primary narcissism and to the humanization of nature?)

14 ". . . He gives them the character of a father" (p. 17). Why? Why are the gods or God himself masculine, while nature is feminine?

Is Freud's claim biological, psychological, or theological? Or is it something else? What was "In the beginning"?

15 According to this account the gods have three great tasks. Why do these tasks change as a culture matures? Freud says the "most gifted people of antiquity" placed Moira above the gods. Why does he not simply use their proper name (he means the Athenian Greeks of the 6th and 5th centuries B.C.)? Why is he so fond of this kind of indirect references in this text? Have we seen him write in this style elsewhere? (Is Moira male or female or something else?)

16 "And thus a store of ideas is created . . ." (p. 18) is Freud's way of announcing his basic thesis. Is it plausible? That is, under what circumstances do most people turn to religion? When both houses of the American Congress convene a new session, opening prayers are offered: Why? What is the usual content of these prayers? Do they entail the kinds of beliefs Freud catalogues on pp. 18–20?

17 Freud was not trained, officially, in the study of religion—though he became well-educated by dint of his own research. But he is not shy about offering this summary of standard Western conceptions of God. Would most academic theologians share these thoughts and these beliefs? Since the middle of the 19th century scholars of religion and official theologians of the various Christian denominations have attempted to amalgamate their beliefs with the teachings and methods of science. Would Freud respect these efforts? Why does he not refer to them or to their authors?

18 Is America "God's own Country"? How would the majority of Americans answer this question? How do most TV preachers understand the relationship between this nation's future and God's will? (What is the shape of worship to which Freud is alluding?) Is Freud an especially "timid" author? Is the next step he proposes to take a small one?

Chapter IV

19 Is Freud worried about the style of the treatise so far? The SE editor refers us to another Freud book, *The Question of Lay Analysis* (1926), in which he used a similar kind of dialogue. Have we seen dialogues anywhere else in Freud? Recall his initial worries about presenting his case histories to a public that might read them as romans à clef. They were not novels, yet did they not have dialogues in them? (Recall the number and use of quotation marks in the three case histories we read above.)

20 Is Freud especially adept at rendering dialogues? What aspects of his profession would prepare him and his students for this kind of

labor? Why would Freud say that he will write the dialogue of an opponent who is mistrustful? What state of mind did he hope his listeners to the *Introductory Lectures* would manifest, particularly at the beginning? Around what kinds of issues does it appear Freud feels most comfortable with the dialogue form of presentation? (Here it would pay one to read carefully the 1926 text on lay analysis in SE 20.)

21 His opponent objects to Freud's use of the verb "created" to describe the way cultures manufactured their religious ideas. What is his objection? With whom would most religious persons agree? How do cultures explain the origin of their sacred institutions and their sacred books? For example, what is the standard Jewish belief about the origin of the Torah? And how do orthodox Christians explain the origins of the New Testament? And how do Mormons understand the origins of their Book of Mormon? Must religious groups maintain these kinds of beliefs? Can Freud contemplate the possibility of a group being both religious (in his sense of that term) and not claiming a divine sanction for its sacred texts?

22 After responding to the charge that the humanization of nature should come as no suprise, Freud repeats his remarks about this "peculiarity" (p. 22) of human thought. Is this fair to his opponent? Had not the latter just said that religious thought is not peculiar at all? In fact, Freud himself appears to argue that *all* cultures manifest some form of religion. And if this is so how could it be a peculiar thing in any manner?

23 How does the distinction between manifest and latent motives, a distinction we saw first in his lectures on dreams, serve him in his attempt to connect this essay with his remarks on totemism in the previous two? Does Freud argue against the possibility of any advance in religious thinking? Does he believe that psychoanalysis will permit us to solve every problem in the history of religions? On the other hand, does he believe that the scientific study of religion can proceed without attending to psychoanalytic findings?

24 "Thus his longing for a father is a motive identical with his need for protection against the consequences of his human weakness" (p. 24). Why? Freud carries out the ontogeny–phylogeny analogy we saw developed in "The Uncanny." In that essay he said some people, including himself, no longer manifested a propensity toward having uncanny experiences. If this is true, does it follow that there might be a corresponding development, a maturation, at the level of culture? The Wolf Man was devout, peculiarly devout one might say, as a boy, yet not so as a young man. What changed? Does Freud hint at a corresponding change in the development of cultural expectations and cultural institutions like the church?

Chapter V

25   Freud begins this chapter as if it were part of a textbook, in the previous chapters of which he had laid down the groundwork for the formulations and definitions that now appear. But is it a textbook and has he laid down such foundations? After offering an exceptionally conventional definition of religious ideas (p. 25), he describes a "very remarkable" experience he himself had years before. Although he adds quickly that he will not lay too much stress upon this example, ought we to agree? Given the validity of the principle of psychic determinism what kinds of questions ought we to ask of this episode and Freud's reasons for including it in this chapter?

26   Most teachings that require belief, both those of science and schoolboy geography, admit of some form of verification. Is this true of religious teachings? Outline the three answers Freud says are typically given in rebuttal of challenges to religious truths. Why is the third an obvious target for psychoanalytic investigations? Have many brilliant intellects broken down over the conflict between the claims of religion and those of science? Are there similar breakdowns over other debates in the natural or social sciences? Given what we know of conflicts typical to neurotics, who also suffer "breakdowns," what kinds of issues must the conflict between the two sets of claims entail? (Consider Freud's emphasis upon the primal ancestors on p. 26.)

27   He then summarizes three possible lines of defense (though his interlocutor is strangely silent in these pages). Are any of them particularly powerful or persuasive to Freud, or to you? Are these the only or the best arguments available to the defenders of religion? Freud refers to one contemporary thinker, Vaihinger (1922). Why does he not refer to the numerous theologians who had also addressed themselves to these issues and who had advanced subtle and, some say, sophisticated counter-arguments?

Chapter VI

28   In this crucial chapter Freud advances his most contentious notion about religion. However, before doing that in the second paragraph he completes his cataloguing of religious claims. Are these trivial? Are the feelings they convey and the hopes they entail silly or products only of the most infantile of desires? The great philosopher Kant once spoke of three great questions to which all serious philosophy addressed itself. How are those three questions related to the wishes Freud describes in this chapter?

29   ". . . All of them are illusions and insusceptible of proof" (p. 31).

Why are they illusions and not simply false or mistaken beliefs? How is it that some illusions have turned out to be correct? Given Freud's definition of this central term, is it correct to say that neurotic patients suffer mainly from their illusions? What is the "reality value" of Dora's unconscious beliefs? Is it correct to say that the Wolf Man's unconscious ideas about his parent's sexual habits were illusions? Or were they something else?

30 Although he did not use this term in a technical manner, Freud discussed the nature of illusion in *Group Psychology*. Where? That is, what aspects of the leader–follower relationship are most likely based upon illusions? And which aspects of being in love manifest a similar reliance upon this human propensity?

31 Freud's tone changes dramatically on p. 32. There he uses the term "sacred" twice, once to describe religious questions, and then to describe a person's relationship to the truth. Is he sincere in both instances? Is one ironic and the other not? In the same paragraph he refers to philosophers of religion (among whom we can include most theologians) who attempt to integrate their rational beliefs with the claims of religion. What are Freud's feelings about such integrative attempts? What kind of religion is he willing to respect and which kind receives his abuse? Who are among the "mighty personalities" of religious doctrine? (Freud's answer to this question is contained in the last text we consider in our common reading.)

32 Is "humble acquiescence" (p. 32) an achievement or a failure? What kind of persons would most likely exhibit this form of humility? Is humility a religious virtue or an "irreligious" one according to the argument of this chapter? And according to you? Does Freud pretend to assess the final truth value of religious claims? Would he have chosen to raise his own children within a religious tradition or would he have abjured it altogether? If the latter, why is he so interested in the claims and nature of religion at all?

33 Were our ancestors "wretched, ignorant, and downtrodden" (p. 33)? Is this the usual way people speak of their ancestors or the way nations portray their forefathers? How might one use the concept of the narcissism of minor differences to explain the grandeur which most societies ascribe to those who went before them? How do Jews and Christians, for example, portray the first communities of their respective faiths? Do they too believe that their ancestors could not have solved all these difficult riddles? Why do most American fundamentalist preachers refer to "New Testament Christianity" as an ideal toward which they strive and against which they judge the current church and current social structures?

Chapter VII

34   Freud lets his interlocutor return in this chapter and challenge the
      equation of religion and mass illusion. Are his opponent's argu-
      ments in favor of religion common to those who wish to defend
      religion against its despisers? That is, are they simply emotional
      reactions which Freud ascribes to a straw man, or might one find
      that a number of religious and lay authorities hold to them as
      well? Who, for example? Is it true, by the way, that the one per-
      son Freud can harm by publishing this book is himself? What
      about all those fine intellects that have broken down over the
      conflict between religion and science?

35   "In point of fact psycho-analysis is a method of research, an impar-
      tial instrument, like the infinitesimal calculus, as it were" (p. 36). Is
      this a perfect analogy? (Note that calculus was among Newton's
      great inventions—why would Freud employ it in his analogy here?)
      Is his attack upon religion not dependent upon his own discoveries
      about the origin of "uncanny" feelings, for example? Do "defenders
      of religion" make use of psychoanalytic methods and theory? Do
      Freud's fundamental theory of mental operations, as well as his
      basic theory of the formation of ideals, have no bearing upon the
      truth-value of religious beliefs?

36   How does Freud know that the number of people dissatisfied with
      our civilization is "appallingly large" (p. 37)? What kinds of clinical
      evidence might he draw upon here in order to support this claim?
      (David Hume, by the way, did not publish his attacks upon the
      proofs for the existence of God—why?) To which Russian novelist is
      he referring on pp. 37–38? How is the question of God's existence
      treated in his novels? (See Freud's ascerbic remarks upon this same
      novelist in his 1928 essay in SE 21.)

37   What is the scientific "spirit" (p. 38)? Why would Freud use this
      term? (Spirit is related to the Latin term spiritus, which in turn is
      related to the Greek term pneuma; both these latter terms appear
      in the Christian terms for the Holy Ghost [or Holy Spirit].) Is it
      true that "civilization has little to fear from educated people and
      brain workers" (p. 39)? How do all communist and most other
      nations as well treat such workers?

Chapter VIII

38   Who is the modern counterpart to St. Boniface, and what forms
      of superstition is he rooting out? This chapter is particularly
      important for understanding Freud's conception of ethics. And
      what is that conception? Are ethical truths discovered in nature?
      Are they revealed by God or by one of his emissaries? Or are they

entirely arbitrary fabrications of the ruling classes or a priestly clan? *Are* all religious ethical demands "rigid" and unchangeable (p. 41)? Is there a state or society that does not claim its fundamental ethical norms are essential truths?

39 Freud immediately recaps his primal horde theory: Why? That is, why does it make sense for him to repeat that theory in this context? Why is he driven to hold that there was an actual primal father, and actual sons, and they actually killed the father? Indeed, how do the most sacred portions of both Jewish and Christian religions support this claim?

40 ". . . The pathology of the individual does not supply us with a fully valid counterpart" (p. 43). Why not? Is the analogy of religion and obsessional neurosis limited because it too closely assimilates religion with a form of mental illness? That is, is Freud restricting his claims out of a feeling of deference to the positive values of religion? If this is so how ought we to understand his remark that devout persons are spared the task of creating personal neuroses (p. 44)? Is this true: Do you know of counterexamples or of persons who are both devout and neurotic?

41 Freud returns to the theme of historical truth when he compares the education of children with the education of the race. If this new analogy is to hold good, what must be true, again, about the actual events that gave rise to the process of civilization? What does he mean by "symbolic disguisings of the truth"? (On the question of Freud's use of the term "symbol" see our discussion of his dream theory). If his other analogy, between analytic treatment and education, is to hold good as well what must we conclude about the usual results of analytic treatment? (See the two articles referred to on p. 44, and see Freud's famous essay on the curative efficacy of psychoanalysis, "Analysis Terminable and Interminable" [1937].)

Chapter IX

42 Freud reintroduces his opponent. But this time he gives him a long speech. Of the four major criticisms leveled against him with which does Freud not deal? "You have said yourself that religion is more than an obsessional neurosis. But you have not dealt with this other side of it" (p. 46). What is the other side? Why does Freud invoke the example of the anthropologist measuring the cranial index of a foreign people? Both *Totem and Taboo* and *Group Psychology* contain extended theories of the origin and usefulness of religion. What must be true if, as Freud holds, a civilization no longer requires them? That is, what needs must be

met minimally if a Father religion is no longer required? What part might psychoanalysis itself play in this phylogenetic event?

43 Is the psychological ideal the "primacy of the intellect" (p. 48)? Was this ideal evident in the three case histories? Is Freud pro- or anti-feminine in this passage: Is it still true that females are subjected to more suppression and repression of their sexual instincts than are males? What does the phrase "thinking like a woman" bring to mind?

44 What has the American experiment with prohibition got to do with the effects of religious ideas upon the maturation of children? Religion is a kind of infantilism according to this text, yet infants and children manifest a "radiant intelligence" which is soon snuffed out by the combined forces of parental suppression and religious instruction. What permits Freud to value one form of childish behavior and to devalue another?

45 The style of Freud's writing in these final pages is worth remarking upon. Have we seen a similar rhetoric elsewhere employed? "Of what use to them is the mirage of wide acres in the moon, whose harvest no one has ever yet seen?" (p. 50). If we treat this and the sentence which follows it as dream images, what kinds of associations and to what form of literature are they related? To what kinds of texts is this kind of language restricted usually? Why would Freud find it useful to quote the two lines from Heine?

Chapter X

46 "If you want to expel religion from our European civilization, you can only do it by means of another system of doctrines; and such a system would from the outset take over all the psychological characteristics of religion . . . for its own defence" (p. 51). This is a much more sophisticated argument for it allows Freud his major claims about religion, yet appears to also force him to demonstrate where or how a non-religious society might function. How is it related to his earlier question, in chapter IX, about the French Revolution?

47 Freud's opponent, perhaps sensing victory, now moves forward and invokes Freud's own theory of the task of civilization: Why is latency that time in which a child must bend to the dictates of civilization? (What characterized the Wolf Man's religious behavior during his latency period?) Following the immense surge of enthusiasm for psychoanalytic ideas in the late '20s and '30s in both Europe and the United States a period of reaction set in; many accused Freud of attempting to replace religion with psychoanalytic doctrines. Why might this seem true? (Why is it, as

Roy Schafer, a noted psychoanalyst has said, that there are no institutes for Darwinian studies alongside the institutes for psychoanalysis?)

48 "If experience should show—not to me, but to others after me, who think as I do—that we have been mistaken, we will give up our expectations" (p. 53). Is this true? Note that most critics of Freud accuse him precisely of not giving up his most cherished ideas, even in the face of evidence contrary to them. Recall to mind some episodes in the three case histories where Freud found himself confronted with a fact that appeared to be contrary to his expectations: How did he respond to it? Should we distinguish Freud's adherence to certain principles, like that of psychic determinism, from his adherence to particular claims? Did Freud change his mind? (Is he, by the way, completely hostile to religion? Does he despise it?)

49 In the midst of his passionate rebuttals Freud alludes to a psychological truth which itself is of sufficient magnitude to guarantee that religious doctrines cannot persist into the infinite future. What is that truth? He hints at it in his remarks about the design of the "mental apparatus" (p. 55). This quality of the mental apparatus finds its counterpart in the less-than-omnipotent God "Logos" (see the SE editor's footnote on p. 54). We spoke of Freud's love of the truth in the introduction to this study: What forces will guarantee that that truth will not disappear? In other words, what must Freud believe about the ontological structure of the human world such that he can say that the voice of the intellect is a soft one, but it does not rest till it has gained a hearing? A more important question now presents itself to us: What clinical evidence can one draw upon to support (or refute) this fundamental belief? If our reading of the three case histories reveals no systematic evidence in favor of the small voice of the intellect, can one say that Freud's opinions are psychoanalytic theorems?

Freud concludes this manifesto with a eulogy to the claims of science and a prediction of its eventual triumph over the realms now ruled by religion. However, he did not abandon the problem of religion. He returned to it in his masterful essay on civilization (*Civilization and Its Discontents*), and at the end of his life in three essays about the greatest Jewish hero: Moses.

Moses and Monotheism: Three Essays (1939)

The SE editors point out that this collection of essays is unlike anything Freud wrote, before or after. This fact will not be disputed by honest readers who, having enjoyed the style of Freud's earlier writings, will be surprised by his repeated hesitations, falterings, and lapses. Yet it remains a great book, particularly for those who wish to comprehend Freud's fascination with religion. The SE editors also refer us to Jones's excellent discussion of the text in the third volume of his biography (the pages are 362–374, not those indicated in the SE "Editor's Note" on p. 5).

I: Moses an Egyptian

1   The SE editors also tell us that Freud's original title for the work was "The Man Moses, a Historical Novel." Why would he have considered this title appropriate? Recall our discussion of the three case histories, especially the introduction to "Dora." How did Freud treat the question of his novelistic skills then? Many of his readers, even those sympathetic to him, remarked upon the literary qualities of his reports: Why did he object strenuously to such analogies? What has occurred in between these two periods?

2   The first sentence is a famous declaration. What power or authority can deprive a people of their hero? Given Moses' stature in both Jewish and Christian beliefs, what corresponding authority must Freud be willing to assume for himself if he is to carry out this great task? Might this be a source of his hesitation? Our question becomes even more significant when we recall that Freud had begun this essay and then published it as Hitler ascended to absolute power. Like most sensible people, he realized that Hitler's manifest aims included that of destroying the Jewish race. Furthermore, by the time Freud had reached the safety of England and acquiesced in the printing of the three essays in a single book, he had already lost a large part of his family to the Nazis. Why then would he go ahead and publish a critical book, based upon speculations, about this central Jewish figure?

3   "Possibly the notion that the man Moses might have been anything but a Hebrew seemed too monstrous" (p. 9). Why? That is, why would Freud use the term monstrous here to indicate the possible emotional reasons why the majority of historians and scientific scholars missed this obvious interpretation of Moses' name? And why is Freud so insistent upon referring to Moses as the man Moses? Why would it fall to psychoanalysts like himself and Otto Rank (pp. 10–12) to uncover this obvious fact?

4   Indeed, how might Freud go on to argue that the nearly universal willingness to overlook this fact is a sure sign of the presence of severe repression? And why would it only be the minority of readers who will be able to follow out his reasoning? After summarizing Rank's major findings Freud says the story of Moses

differs from the norm in one essential respect. What is that respect and why does Freud emphasize the importance of recognizing three families?

5   If Freud's reconstruction is correct, why does it follow that there must be an Egyptian legend in which the king is warned, by some uncanny messenger, that his royal son is to become a threat to him? "The exposure in the water was at its correct point in the story . . ." (p. 15), but the Jews changed the remainder. Why? Have we come across similar reversals either in dreams or in neurotic fantasies?

6   While he is aware of the speculative quality of all his conjectures thus far, Freud does not hesitate to list the possible results his inquiry may afford us: an explanation of the peculiar history of the Jews and the origins of monotheistic religion itself. He concludes by arguing against his current position for it lacks a "second firm fact" with which to defend these immense conclusions. Does he ever offer us a fact which a neutral observer could call "firm"? To answer these last questions we must turn to the second essay.

II: If Moses Was an Egyptian

7   Freud says many previous scholars had observed that the official Jewish and Christian understandings of Moses' name and birth are improbable. He added to these critical opinions by drawing upon the "myth of exposure" analysis he and Rank had advanced twenty years before. Could anyone else have used this kind of information? That is, is it possible to conceive of a scholar using the methods of comparative religion to advance a similar thesis without the use of psychoanalytic theory? If Freud's project is to gain any validity at all what unstated principle must he rely upon in order to use 20th-century psychological theory to analyze the motives of a man and his followers who lived three thousand years ago?

8   The entire style of these essays is determined by the hypothetical mode: if (as is evident in the title of this second part). It is worth noting what kinds of "ifs" Freud is willing to contemplate and what kinds of "ifs" he is not. For example, why can we not say, "if Moses was divinely inspired," or, "if God appeared to Moses (the Hebrew) and gave him great powers and the skill to lead his people"?

9   Are the differences between early Jewish religion and the Egyptian religion of the time "of the most violent" contrast (p. 19)? Why does Freud use this kind of rhetoric in these few opening pages? (Note that they introduce us in part to the "remarkable"

fact that there were two great forms of Egyptian religion.) Why is Freud not willing to grant that Moses' form of monotheism could have originated with him alone? Is this a persuasive argument? Are there any historically valid examples of single persons creating entirely new religions?

10   Did monotheism arise elsewhere in the world at this or any previous time? This is an immensely difficult question to answer since it requires one to survey a huge literature in the comparative study of religion. If one found that there were neither contemporary nor earlier forms of monotheism, would that strengthen Freud's argument? Why is he convinced that so "sublime" a thought as monotheism could not originate except at the end of a long tradition of speculation and within the confines of an immense empire like that of the Eighteenth Dynasty? Is there a consistent relationship between a culture's theological structures and its political structures? How could one go about answering this kind of question?

11   After linking the Jewish rite of circumcision with its Egyptian precursor, Freud has to face the apparent fact that his speculations will not fit into the traditionally accepted date of the Exodus (pp. 29–31). But he refuses to budge from his claim that Moses *must* have been an Egyptian follower of the great monotheistic King, Akhenaten, whose personal and political catastrophe had involved him. Indeed, "perhaps he was at that time Governor of the frontier province (Goshen) in which certain Semitic tribes had settled" (p. 29). Why is Freud willing to suffer this immense criticism so early in his exposition? (Have we seen him exhibit a similar obstinacy before? Where?)

12   Returning to the question of Moses' activities, it would appear that another historian, Eduard Meyer, has shown that the Moses associated with the volcano god, Yahweh, was a shepherd. If this is so it would follow that Freud's portrait of a regal Egyptian Moses cannot be accurate. But Freud escapes this snare too—how? At this point in one's reading it may prove valuable to keep a time chart of Freud's major contentions; e.g., on p. 37 he places the murder of the Egyptian Moses much earlier than the unification of the kindred tribes.

13   Freud was very fond of antiquities, especally Egyptian ones. Given what we have learned about such affections in other people, what can we suppose must be true of this kind of sublimation? That is, Freud himself has taught us that it is precisely those things that fascinate one, that one finds uncanny, which are the sublime representatives of one's archaic wishes. We saw Freud advance this thesis in the *Introductory Lectures* in the chapters on dream interpretation. Hence, we may ask what kinds of wishes

and archaic fantasies might a lifelong fascination with Egyptian antiquities represent? (A photograph of Freud with part of his collection of Egyptian statues may be found on the frontispiece of SE 23 and frontispiece of SE 12.)

14 In the midst of these fresh speculations Freud says a number of times that it was the Egyptian branch of the federated tribes which were the more cultured and educated. Why does he rely upon this claim? How does he, in turn, connect it to the ambiguous status traditionally attributed to the Levites? (Is it true in other historical epochs that later fusions are frequently undone, even if that original unification occurred many hundreds of years before? Is it true in modern times as well? Are there similar dissolutions obvious in individuals?

15 "The text, however, as we possess it to-day will tell us enough about its own vicissitudes" (p. 43). Where else have we seen Freud advance this kind of argument? What special insights into the process of distortion should psychoanalytic training afford one? (Note that Freud attributes other major cultural advances to the Mosaic Egyptians as well: Why to them and not to the original Semitic tribes themselves?)

16 Why is Freud so keen to point out what he claims are puzzling and incomprehensible passages in the Bible texts? How does the presence of so many distorted sayings, incoherent legends and contradictions within the sacred texts support his basic argument? Recall our discussion of Dora's account of her illness: What particular features of that narration were undeniable indicators of her neurotic character?

17 Freud concludes this sixth section of the second essay with the argument that the new Semitic religion that was grafted onto that of the Man Moses reverted back to that earliest "Jewish" form. What historical evidence can he bring forth in support of this fantastic claim? And what evidence from the psychology of the individual might he adduce to supplement, at least, that historical evidence? In other words, do we have any other examples of this kind of regressive restoration from either distinct historical epochs or the three case histories?

18 After summarizing his argument and offering a minimal chronology Freud turns toward the Jews of his day, from whom he has just taken their greatest hero and of whom he has just accused of a form of deicide, and offers them some consolation. What is that consolation and is Freud as disdainful of it as he appeared to be of the Christian doctrines which required one to hate those who were not fellow believers? His last remarks, on pp. 52–53, include a reference to the importance of great men and the "sacrilege"

one commits against human life if one refuses to recognize "spiritual" aims. Are these typical of one who hates his religion or its history?

III: Moses, His People, and Monotheist Religion

Part I

A book which aims to introduce the serious student to an understanding of some aspects of Freud's thought ought not to end on a note of confusion and disarray. And, as the SE editors point out, Freud's mind did not deteriorate. After completing these three essays on Moses he wrote the initial parts of his last text, *An Outline of Psychoanalysis* (SE 23, 1940), which is a vivid and concise discussion of his science. Yet this third and much the longest section of his study of Moses is hardly concise. But it is vivid and honest. It represents Freud the man in an especially direct way since he refers to his own state (and that of his family) numerous times in the work. The clever slur against the Germans of his day (p. 54) is not the product of a confused mind.

19 It sometimes appears as if Freud means only to advance an analogy between his study of individuals and these essays on a group phenomenon like religion. But are these analogies only? If so, why is Freud so concerned about publishing his study (cf. pp. 58 and 72ff.)?

20 After recapitulating his story, and giving us an even grander portrait of the monotheistic Pharaoh, Akhenaten, Freud introduces a new dimension to his argument: latency. Freud's literary devices and rhetoric are important aspects of his argument. For example, he says that the return of Mosaic (Egyptian) monotheism to the Hebrews is a "remarkable" fact (p. 69). Why? Why is the return of this supposedly repressed mode of religion a sign of its actual historical existence?

21 The bulk of this essay is an attempt to argue for the existence of actual events, which are then remembered symbolically in the forms of religious rituals and beliefs. Have we seen Freud address this question in his essays on individual neurotics? (Why does he say his argument seeks to unite group psychology and individual psychology with the *postulate* of the identity between religion and obsessional neurosis [p. 72]?)

22 Although one may find Freud's exposition of the parallels between the genesis of adult neurosis from infantile precursors and the creation of an advanced religion from earlier forms suggestive, it would appear to falter on one major problem. Some neurotics report "memories" of events in their past, like parental seduction, which

never occurred. Freud had to face this fact early in his career when
he abandoned his original theory that later outbreaks of neurosis
were the results of the reinstigation of sealed-over trauma. If there is
no consistent evidence that all traumatic neuroses have this aetiology, how can Freud employ them as models for historical events?
How do the examples of early Greek legends provide him some aid
in carrying out his proposals?

23 One cannot fault Freud's gumption, for in the next few sections
he succeeds in tying Christianity and its greatest apostle, Paul, to
the murder of Moses and both of those to the primal crime he had
elaborated upon in *Totem and Taboo*. The truth of what psychological principle permits him to do this? For example, how does
he show that one ought to envision Jesus as the return of the Man
Moses? How is the hatred against Jews at bottom a hatred against
Christians? (What is the history of the German Christian churches
in their relation to Hitler and the Nazi regime?)

24 Part E, Difficulties, is an especially crucial part of the reconstruction. Why does he spend so much effort proposing that there must
be memory-traces of actual historical events which survive in a
common archaic heritage? How does the latter concept help him
complete the work of *Group Psychology and the Analysis of the
Ego*?

Part II

25 Where else have we read of "tormenting ghosts" in Freud? It was
this kind of ghost that forced him to begin this most awkward
essay again (pp. 103–104). Strictly speaking, what are ghosts and
from whose past and toward what future are they most likely
directed? The SE editor has referred to the special difficulties of
translating Freud's German term *"Geistigkeit."* It means both
spirituality and intellectuality (for example, it occurs in the German expression for the Holy Ghost [another kind of ghost], and in
Hegel's great work, *The Phenomenology of Mind*). Is Freud's use
of the term "spirituality" ironic or does he believe there is something uniquely valuable in the Jewish (and Egyptian!) peoples?

26 In part B, The Great Man, Freud advances his argument for the
special place a great historical person may have in the history of a
people or a nation. Does he deny that social, economic, and political
structures may also play a role in the "overdetermination" of a particular group achieving a significant status? Yet not all powerful
people are great—what particular good must a great leader provide
his (or her) followers? (Does Freud himself fit this requirement?)
Could a woman ever fulfill the same requirement?

27   Why is Freud so concerned to explain the sense of superiority
     which he says characterizes Jews, both of the earliest times and of
     this century? How is the triumph of the Egyptian Moses' ideas
     related to the immense differences Jews traditionally feel exist
     between themselves and their neighbors? (Are these issues still
     alive in our day as they were in the Roman world and in Europe
     in the 1930s?) "In this dichotomy their decision was at least in
     favour of the worthier alternative" (p. 115). Is this an unsupported
     value judgment? Or can Freud call upon psychological theory, if
     not psychological facts, with which he can justify placing intellec-
     tuality above physical development?

28   This question allows us to address Freud's comments on the genesis
     of ethics in part D, The Renunciation of Instinct (pp. 116–122).
     Although he relies upon the terminology and distinctions found in
     The Ego and the Id (1923), a text we have not studied, his discussion
     is not too far removed from that found in a text we do know, *Group
     Psychology*. We have asked if a woman could ever become a Great
     Man, now we can ask if she might ever contribute to the construc-
     tion of the superego. How must Freud answer this question, given
     his distinction between paternity and maternity on p. 118? And
     how is paternity related to the choice of objects and actions which
     shall be "holy" and those that shall be "taboo"?

29   What is "true in religion"? If religious beliefs had neither truth
     nor value, would they persist over thousands of years of history?
     Why is the persistence of religion, especially among the scientifi-
     cally educated, a particular problem for Freud? Was it simply
     Moses' powerful character which imposed itself upon the Jews or
     something else that led to the return of his "spirit"? How does
     Freud account for the interesting fact that a preponderant num-
     ber of intellectuals are Jewish and the remarkable fact that the
     majority of psychoanalysts were and are Jewish?

30   In part F, The Return of the Repressed, Freud offers a rare con-
     sideration of the formation of character. Can the past ever be
     overcome completely? Did any of his patients show that he or she
     could renounce completely the pleasures of childhood and over-
     come the tendency toward repetition of those earliest behaviors
     associated with those pleasures? Is psychoanalytic treatment itself
     a variation of the return of the repressed? Consider Freud's
     laments about his failure with Dora: How were her transference
     wishes themselves replications of the return of the repressed?
     Finally, is sublimation wholly unlike the return of repressed
     wishes?

31   "There is an element of grandeur about everything to do with the
     origin of religion, certainly including the Jewish one, and this is

not matched by the explanations we have hitherto given" (p. 128). Are these the remarks of an implacable foe of religion? Is Freud willing to grant that there are differences of merit between "archaic" religion and monotheism, for example? Does he disagree with "many Jews" (p. 134) who assert that the ethical heights of Judaism are achievements comparable to its championing of monotheism?

32 Finally, Freud does not hestitate to include Paul and Christianity in his grand thesis. How is the latter a son religion? And how is Paul's theology of original sin itself a return of the repressed? "It was as though Egypt was taking vengeance once more on the heir of Akhenaten" (p. 136). Why does Freud say "as though" here? Does he believe this claim in some way? What was the first occasion upon which Egypt took revenge upon the great king? Does Freud believe that Christianity *is* a "forward step" in the development of "intellectuality" (p. 136)? How might Jewish readers of the time in which this essay was first published respond to these final sentiments?   •

REFERENCES

THE WORK OF SIGMUND FREUD

Freud Texts

Abbreviations: International Universities Press = IUP.

Freud, Sigmund, *The Standard Edition of the Complete Psychological Works of Sigmund Freud*. 24 vols. London: Hogarth Press & Institute for Psychoanalysis.

Freud, Sigmund, *Gesammelte Werke*. 18 vols. in 17. Frankfurt am Main: S. Fischer, 1960.

The Concordance to the Standard Edition of the Complete Psychological Works of Sigmund Freud, S. A. Guttman, R. L. Jones, S. M. Parrish. (Eds.). Boston: G. K. Hall, 1980. 6 volumes, 5512 pp.

Freud, Sigmund, *On Aphasia* [1891]. London: Imago Publishing Co., 1953, xv + 105 pp.

Freud, Sigmund, *Cocaine Papers by Sigmund Freud*, R. Byck (Ed.). New York: Stonehill, 1974, xxxix + 414pp.

Freud, Sigmund, *The Origins of Psycho-Analysis: Letters to Wilhelm Fliess, Drafts and Notes: 1887–1902*. M. Bonaparte, A. Freud, E. Kris, (Eds.). New York: Basic Books, 1954, xi + 486 pp.

Abstracts of the Standard Edition of Freud. New York: Jason Aronson, 1974, 315 pp.

"A Pagination Converter Relating the Gesammelte Werke to the Standard Edition of the Complete Psychological Works of Sigmund Freud." G. H. Klumpner and E. S. Wolf. *International Journal of Psycho-Analysis*, 52:207–224.

Reference Aids

Eidelberg, L., (Ed.), *Encyclopedia of Psychoanalysis*. New York: Free Press, 1968, xxxviii + 571 pp.

Fodor, N., and F. Gaynor, *Dictionary of Psychoanalysis*. New York: Philosophical Library, 1950, 208 pp.

Greenberg, Bette, *How to Find Out in Psychiatry: A Guide to Sources of Mental Health Information*. New York: Pergamon Press, 1978, 113pp.

Grinstein, Alexander, *Sigmund Freud's Writings: A Comprehensive Bibliography*. New York: IUP, 1977, 181 pp.

Kiell, Norman, *Psychoanalysis, Psychology, and Literature: A Bibliography*. Madison: University of Wisconsin, 1963, v + 225pp.

Kiell, Norman, *Psychiatry and Psychology in the Visual Arts and Aesthetics: A Bibliography*. Madison, University of Wisconsin, 1965, xiv + 250p.

Laplanche, J. & Pontalis, J., *The Language of Psychoanalysis*. Trans. D. Nicholson-Smith. New York: Norton (orig. 1967).

Marmor, Judd, (Ed.), *Modern Psychoanalysis: New Directions and Perspectives*. New York: Basic Books, 1968, 732 pp.

Moore, Burness and Fine, B.D. (Eds.), *A Glosssary of Psychoanalytic Terms and Concepts*. New York: American Psychoanalytic Association, 1967, 96pp.

Nagera, Humberto (Ed.), *Basic Psychoanalytic Concepts of the Libido Theory*. New York: Basic Books, 1969. 195 pp.

Nagera, Humberto (Ed.), *Basic Psychoanalytic Concepts on Metapsychology, Conflicts, Anxiety and Other Subjects*. New York: Basic Books, 1970, 233pp.

Nagera, Humberto (Ed.), *Basic Psychoanalytic Concepts on the Theory of Dreams*. New York: Basic Books, 1969, 121pp.

Nagera, Humberto (Ed.), *Basic Psychoanalytic Concepts on the Theory of Instincts*. New York: Basic Books, 1971. 136pp.

Rapaport, David, *The Structure of Psychoanalytic Theory*. New York: IUP, 1960, 158pp.

Wolman, B. B. (Ed.), *International Encyclopedia of Psychiatry, Psychology, Psychoanalysis, and Neurology*. New York: Van Nostrand Reinhold, 1977, 12 vols.

Indexes and Reviews

Beit-Hallahmi, B. (Ed.) *Psychoanalysis and Religion: A Bibliography*. Norwood, Pa.: Norwood Editions, 1980, 182pp.

Capps. D.; Rambo, L.; & Ransohoff, P., *Psychology of Religion: A Guide to Information Resources*. Detroit: Gale, 1976, 352pp.

Chicago Institute for Psychoanalysis, *Chicago Psychoanalytic Literature Index*, 1920. 3 vols. Chicago: Chicago Processing Laboratories, 1971.

Freud, Sigmund, *Indexes and Bibliographies*, Standard Edition, vol. 24. A. Richards (Ed.). London: Hogarth Press, 1974.

Grinstein, Alexander, *The Index of Psychoanalytic Writings*. Series 1, vols. 1–5, 1956–1960; Series 2, vols. 6–9, 1964–1966; Series 3, vols. 10–14, 1971–75. New York: IUP.

Hart, H. H., *Conceptual Index of Psychoanalytic Technique and Training.* 5 vols. Croton-on-Hudson: North River Press, 1972.

Journal of the American Psychoanalytic Association, Cumulative Index 1953–1974. New York: IUP, 1976.

Klumper, G. H., "A Review, Comparison and Evaluation of Psychoanalytic Indexes", *Journal of the American Psychoanalytic Association.* (1975) 23:603–642.

Pruyser, Paul, "Sigmund Freud and His Legacy: Psychoanalytic Psychology of Religion." In: *Beyond the Classics.* C. Glock and P. Hammond (Eds.). New York: Harper, 1973, pp. 243–290.

Psychoanalytic Quarterly: Cumulative Index 1932–1966. New York: The Psychoanalytic Quarterly, Inc., 1969.

Rycroft, Charles, *A Critical Dictionary of Psychoanalysis.* London: Penguin, 1972.

ON FREUD THE MAN

Autobiographical and Family Accounts

Bergmann, Martin S, "Moses and the Evolution of Freud's Jewish Identity." *The Israel Annals of Psychiatry and Related Sciences,* (1976) 14:3–26.

Bernays, Anna Freud, "My Brother, Sigmund Freud." *American Mercury,* (1940) 51:335–342.

Engleman, Edmund, *Berggasse 19: Sigmund Freud's Home and Office, Vienna 1938.* [photographs]. New York: Basic Books, 1976, 153pp.

Freud, Martin, *Sigmund Freud: Man and Father.* London and New York: Vanguard Press, 1957, 218pp.

Freud, Sigmund, *An Autobiographical Study.* SE 20:3–74.

Heller, Judith Bernays, "Freud's Mother and Father." *Commentary,* (1956) 21:418–21.

Freud's Letters

Freud, Ernest L., (Ed.), *The Letters of Sigmund Freud and Arnold Zweig.* London: Hogarth, 1970, 190pp.

Freud, Sigmund, *The Freud/Jung Letters: The Correspondence between Sigmund Freud and C. G. Jung.* W. McGuire (Ed.), trans. R. Manheim, R. F. C. Hull. Princeton: Princeton University Press, 1974, xlii + 650pp.

Freud, Sigmund, *Letters.* Selected and ed. by E. L. Freud. New York: Basic Books, 1960, viii + 470.

Freud, Sigmund, *Psychoanalysis and Faith: The Letters of Sigmund Freud and Oskar Pfister.* New York: Basic Books, 1963, 152pp.

Freud, Sigmund and Karl Abraham, *A Psycho-Analytic Dialogue: The Letters of Sigmund Freud and Karl Abraham 1907–1926*. H. C. Abraham and E. L. Freud (Eds.). New York: Basic Books, 1965, xvii + 406pp.

Robson-Scott, W. and E., trans., *Sigmund Freud and Lou Andreas-Salome: Letters*. New York: Harcourt, Brace, Jovanovich, 1972, 244pp.

Shengold, L., "*The Freud/Jung Letters*" in Kanzer, M. and Jules Glen, (Eds.), *Freud and his Self-Analysis*. New York: Jason Aronson, pp.187-201.

Accounts by Friends and Patients

Andreas-Salome, Lou, *Freud Journal of Lou Andreas-Salome*. S. A. Leary, (Ed.). New York: Basic Books, 1964, 211pp.

Binswanger, Ludwig, *Sigmund Freud: Reminiscences of a Friendship*. New York: Grune & Stratton, 1957, 103pp.

Blanton, S., *Diary of my Analysis with Sigmund Freud*. New York: Hawthorn Books, 1971, 141pp.

Doolittle, Hilda, *Tribute to Freud*. Balfour: D. R. Ondine, 1974, xiv + 194pp.

Dorsey, John M., *An American Psychiatrist in Vienna, 1935–1937, and his Sigmund Freud*. Detroit: Center for Health Education, 1976, 213pp.

Gardiner, M., (Ed.), *The Wolf Man and Sigmund Freud*. London: Hogarth, 1972, xiv + 370pp.

Kardiner, A., *My Analysis with Freud*. New York: W. W. Norton, 1977, 123pp.

Reich, Wilhelm, *Reich Speaks of Freud*. M. H. Raphael, (Ed). New York: Noonday, 1967, xvi + 294pp.

Reik, Theodor, *From Thirty Years with Freud*. New York: Farrar & Rinehart, 1940, xi + 241pp.

Ruitenbeek, Hendrik (Ed.), *Freud as We Knew Him*. Detroit: Wayne State University Press, 524pp.

Sachs, Hans, *Freud, Master and Friend*. Cambridge: Harvard University Press, 1945, 195pp.

Weiss, Edoardo, *Sigmund Freud as Consultant*. New York: Intercontinental Medical Books, 1970, vi + 82pp.

Wortis, Joseph, *Fragments of an Analysis with Freud*. Indianapolis: Bobbs-Merrill, 1954, x + 208pp.

Major Biographical Accounts

Brome, Vincent, *Freud and His Early Circle*. New York: Wm. Morrow & Co., 1968, xii + 275pp.

Clark, R. W., *Freud: The Man and the Cause*. New York: Random, 1980, xii + 632pp.

Ellenberger, H., *The Discovery of the Unconscious: The History and Evolution of Dynamic Psychiatry*. New York: Basic Books, 1970, 932pp.

Fromm, Erich, *Sigmund Freud's Mission*. New York: Harper, 1959, 129pp.

Grinstein, Alexander, *On Sigmund Freud's Dreams*. Detroit: Wayne State University Press, 1968, 475pp.

Jones, Ernest, *The Life and Work of Sigmund Freud*. New York: Basic Books, 3 vols., 1953–57.

Jung, Carl, The Freudian Theory of Hysteria (Collected Works vol. 4); The Theory of Psychoanalysis, CW 4; Freud and Jung: Contrasts, CW 4; Sigmund Freud and His Historical Setting, CW 15; In Memory of Sigmund Freud, CW 15. All in: *The Collected Works of C. G. Jung*. Trans. R. F. C. Hull. Princeton: Princeton University Press, 1953–71.

Kanzer, M. and Jules Glen. (Eds.), *Freud and Self-Analysis*, Vol. 1. New York: Jason Aronson, 1979, 308pp.

Kanzer, M. and Jules Glen. (Eds.), *Freud and His Patients*, Vol. II. New York: Jason Aronson, 1980, 452pp.

Mahoney, Patrick, *Freud as a Writer*. New York: IUP 1982, 235pp.

Robert, Marthe, *From Oedipus to Moses: Freud's Jewish Identity*. Trans. R. Manheim. Garden City, NY: Anchor, 1976, 229pp.

Ruitenbeek, Hendrik M., *Freud and America*. New York: Macmillan, 1966, 192pp.

Schur, Max, *Freud: Living and Dying*. New York: IUP, 1972, xi + 587pp.

PSYCHOANALYSIS: HISTORY & THEORY

History of Psychoanalysis

Alexander, Franz and Helen Ross, *The Impact of Freudian Psychiatry*. Chicago: University of Chicago Press, 1952, 305pp.

Alexander, Franz and S. Eisenstein, *Psychoanalytic Pioneers*. New York: Basic Books, 1966, xvii + 616pp.

Amacher, Peter, *Freud's Neurological Education and Its Influence on Psychoanalytic Theory*. New York: IUP, 1965, 93pp.

Bettelhiem, Bruno, *Freud and Man's Soul*. New York: Knopf, 1983.

Brandell, G., *Freud: A Man of His Century*. Sussex: Harvester Press, 1979, xi + 110.

Burnham, John C. *Psychoanalysis and American Medicine: 1894–1918*. New York: IUP, 1967, 249pp.

Chabot, C. Barry, *Freud on Schreber: Psychoanalytic Theory and the*

Critical Act. Amherst: University of Massachusetts, 1982, 171pp.

Chertok, Leon and de Saussure, Raymond, *The Therapeutic Revolution: From Mesmer to Freud.* New York: Brunner/Mazel, 1979, xiii + 226pp.

Decker, Hannah S., *Freud in Germany: Revolution and Reaction in Science 1893–1907.* Psychological Issues (Monograph 41). New York: IUP, 1979, 360pp.

Fine, R., *A History of Psychoanalysis.* New York: Columbia University Press, 1979, 686pp.

Gifford, G. E., Jr., (Ed.), *Psychoanalysis,Psychotherapy, and the New England Medical Scene, 1894–1944.* New York: Science History Publications, 1978, xxiii + 438pp.

Hale, Nathan G., *Freud and the Americans: The Beginnings of Psychoanalysis in the United States, 1876–1917,* (Vol. I) New York: Oxford, 1971, xvi + 574pp.

Klein, Dennis B., *Jewish Origins of the Psychoanalytic Movement.* New York: Praeger, 1981, xvi + 198pp.

Levi, K., *Freud's Early Psychology of the Neuroses: A Historical Perspective.* Pittsburgh: University of Pittsburgh Press, 1978, 314pp.

Lewis, Helen B., *Freud and Modern Psychiatry.* New York: Plenum, 1981, 247pp.

Minutes of the Vienna Psychoanalytic Society. 4 vols. H. Nunberg and E. Federn (Eds.); trans. M. Nunberg. New York: IUP, 1962–1975.

Munroe, Ruth, *Schools of Psychoanalytic Thought: An Exposition, Critique, and Attempt at Integration.* New York: Holt, Rinehart, and Winston, 1955, xvi + 670pp.

Nelson, Benjamin, (Ed.), *Freud and the Twentieth Century.* Gloucester: Peter Smith, 1958, 314pp.

Norton, Frederic, *A Nervous Splendor: Vienna 1888/1889.* New York: Penguin, 1979, x + 340pp.

Roazen, Paul, *Freud and His Followers.* New York: Knopf, 1975, 599 pp.

Robinson, Paul A., *The Freudian Left: Wilhelm Reich, Geza Roheim, Herbert Marcuse.* New York: Harper & Row, 1969, ix + 253 pp.

Sherman, M. H., *Psychoanalysis in America.* Springfield, Illinois: Charles C. Thomas, 1966, xii + 518 pp.

Stewart, W. A., *Psychoanalysis: The First Ten Years.* New York: Macmillan, 1967, 225pp.

Wyss, Dieter, *Depth Psychology: A Critical History.* New York: Norton, 1966, 568pp.

Whyte, L. L., *The Unconscious Before Freud.* New York: Basic Books, 1960, xi + 219pp.

Surveys, Critiques, Summaries

Brenner, Charles, *An Elementary Textbook of Psychoanalysis.* Garden City, New York: Doubleday Anchor, 1955, x + 224pp.

The Course of Life: Psychoanalytic Contributions Toward Understanding Personality Development. S. I. Greenspan and G. H. Pollock (Eds.). 3 vols. U.S. Department of Health and Human Services. DHHS Publication No. 80–786.

Fancher, Raymond E., *Psychoanalytic Psychology: The Development of Freud's Thought.* New York: Norton, 1973, xi + 241 pp.

Farrell, B. A., *The Standing of Psychoanalysis.* Oxford: OUP, 1981, 240 pp.

Feffer, Melvin, *The Structure of Freudian Thought: The Problem of Immutability and Discontinuity in Developmental Theory.* New York: IUP, 1982, 298pp.

Fenichel, Otto, *The Psychoanalytic Theory of Neurosis.* New York: Norton, 1945, 703pp.

Fine, Ruben, *The Psychoanalytic Vision: A Controversial Reappraisal of the Freudian Revolution.* New York: Free Press, 1981, xiv + 577 pp.

Fliess, R., (Ed.), *The Psycho-Analytic Reader: An Anthology of Essential Papers with Critical Introductions.* New York: IUP, 1948, xvii + 358pp.

Freeman, Lucy, *Exploring the Mind of Man: Sigmund Freud and the Age of Psychology.* New York: Grosset & Dunlap, 1969, 150pp.

Freud: A Collection of Critical Essays. Richard Wollheim, (Ed.), Garden City, New York: Anchor Books, xv + 416 pp.

Gedo, John, and George Pollock, (Eds.), *Freud: The Fusion of Science and Humanism: The Intellectual History of Psychoanalysis.* New York: IUP, 1976, 445pp.

Hall, Calvin S., *A Primer of Freudian Psychology.* Cleveland: World Books, 1954, 137 pp.

Holt, R. R., "On Reading Freud." In: *Abstracts of the Standard Edition of Freud.* New York: Jason Aronson, 1974, pp. 1–79, 315pp.

Hook, S., (Ed.), *Psychoanalysis, Scientific Method, and Philosophy.* New York: NYU Press, 1959, xii + 370 pp.

Holzman, Philip S., *Psychoanalysis and Psychopathology.* New York: McGraw-Hill, 1970, xvi + 204 pp.

Jahoda, Marie, *Freud and the Dilemmas of Psychology.* New York: Basic Books, 1977, 186 pp.

Johnston, Thomas E, *Freud and Political Thought*. New York: Citadel Press, 1965, 160 pp.

Lewis, Helen Block, *Freud and Modern Psychology: The Emotional Basis of Mental Illness*. New York: Plenum, 1981, 240 pp.

Masling, Joseph, (Ed.), *Empirical Studies of Psychoanalytic Theories*. Hillside, N.J.: Analytic Press, 1983.

Pribram, K., and Gill, Merton, *Freud's Project Re-Assessed*. London: Hutchinson, 1976, 192 pp.

Ricoeur, Paul, *Freud and Philosophy*. New Haven: Yale, 1970, 573pp.

Rieff, Philip, *Freud: The Mind of the Moralist*. New York: Doubleday & Co., 1959, xvi + 397pp.

Roazen, Paul, *Freud: Political and Social Thought*. New York: Random House, 1968, xii + 322 pp.

Roazen, Paul, (Ed.), *Sigmund Freud*. Englewood Cliffs, N.J.: Prentice-Hall, 1973, 186 pp.

Rosenblatt, A. D., and J. T. Thickstun, *Modern Psychological Concepts in a General Psychology*. New York: IUP, 1972, xiv + 348pp.

Sarnoff, Irving, *Testing Freudian Concepts: An Experimental Social Approach*. New York: Springer, 1971, 276 pp.

Sears, R. R., *Survey of Objective Studies of Psychoanalytic Concepts*. New York: Social Science Research Council, 1943, vii + 156pp.

Shakow, D., and Rapaport, D., *The Influence of Freud on American Psychology*. New York: IUP,1964, 243pp.

Sherwood, Michael, *The Logic of Explanation in Psychoanalysis*. New York: Academic Press, 1969, vii + 276pp.

Strupp, Hans, *An Introduction to Freud and Modern Psychoanalysis*. Woodbury, N.Y.: Barron's Educational Series, 1967, 101 pp.

Sulloway, Frank, *Freud: Biologist of the Mind*. New York: Basic Books, 612 pp.

Trilling, Lionel, *Freud and the Crisis of Our Culture*. Boston: Beacon, 59 pp.

Wollheim, Richard, *Sigmund Freud*. New York: Viking Press, 1971, xix + 292pp.

Wollheim, Richard & James Hopkins, (Eds.), *Philosophical Essays on Freud*. Cambridge: Cambridge University Press, 1982.

Yankelovich, Daniel, and William Barrett, *Ego and Instinct: the Psychoanalytic View of Human Nature—Revised*. New York: Vintage Books, 1970, xiv + 494 pp.

JOURNALS AND PERIODICALS

Periodicals frequently cited and most available to American readers are: Bulletin of the Menninger Clinic, Journal of the American Psychoanalytic Association, International Journal of Psycho-Analysis, Psychoanalytic

Study of the Child, and the monograph series, Psychological Issues. The city where the journal is edited currently and the year of its initial volume appear after each title.

Abstracts of the Psychoanalytic Study of the Child, Ed. C. L. Rothgeb. US Department of Health, Education, and Welfare. DHEW Publication No. 73–9007. 1972.

American Imago, Detroit, 1943.

American Journal of Orthopsychiatry, New York, 1930.

American Journal of Psychoanalysis, New York, 1941.

The Annual of Psychoanalysis, Chicago Institute for Psychoanalysis, 1973.

The Annual Survey of Psychoanalysis, New York, 1959.

Bulletin of the Association for Psychoanalytic Medicine, New York, 1961.

Bulletin of the Menninger Clinic, Topeka, 1936.

Contemporary Psychoanalysis, New York, 1964.

Hillside Journal of Clinical Psychiatry, New York, 1979.

The International Journal of Psycho-Analysis, London, 1919.

International Journal of Psychoanalytic Psychotherapy, New York, 1971.

International Review of Psychoanalysis, London, 1974.

The Journal of the American Academy of Psychoanalysis, New York, 1973.

Journal of the American Psychoanalytic Association, New York, 1953.

Journal of the Philadelphia Association of Psychoanalysis, Philadelphia, 1974.

Journal of Psychoanalytic Anthropology, New York, 1978.

Journal of Psycho-History, New York, 1973.

Journal of the History of Medicine and Allied Sciences, Minneapolis, 1945.

Modern Psychoanalysis, New York, 1976.

Psychiatry, Washington, D. C., 1938.

Psychoanalysis and Contemporary Thought, New York, 1972.

Psychoanalytic Inquiry: A Topical Journal for Mental Health Professionals, New York, 1982.

The Psychoanalytic Quarterly, New York, 1916.

The Psychoanalytic Review, New York, 1913.

The Psychoanalytic Study of the Child, London, 1945.

The Psychoanalytic Study of Society, New Haven, 1947.

Psychohistory Review, New York, 1971.

Psychological Issues, New York, 1959.

Review of Psychoanalytic Books, New York, 1982.

Samiksa, Indian Journal of Psychoanalysis, Calcutta, 1947.

Scandinavian Psychoanalytic Review, Copenhagen, 1978.
Sigmund Freud House Bulletin, Vienna, 1975.

Foreign Language Journals

Dynamische Psychiatrie, Berlin, 1968.
Etudes Freudiennes, Paris, 1969.
Fortschritte der Psychonalyse (Progress of Psychoanalysis), Goettingen, 1964.
Jahrbuch der Psychoanalyse, Berne, Switzerland, 1964.
Nouvelle Revue de Psychanalyse, Paris, 1974.
Psychanalyse a L'Universite, Paris, 1975.
Psyche, Stuttgart, 1947.
Revista de Psicoanalisis, Buenos Aires, 1943.
Revue Francaise de Psychanalyse, Paris, 1927.
Rivista di Psicoanalisi, Rome, 1955.
Zeitschrift fur Psychosomatische Medizin und Psychoanalyse, Goettingen, 1954.

INDEX